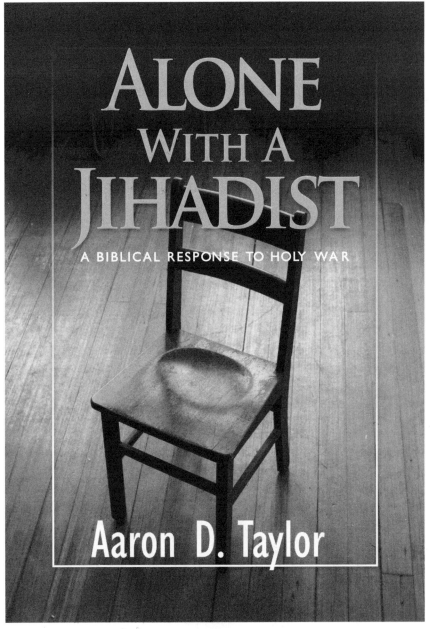

ALONE
WITH A
JIHADIST

A BIBLICAL RESPONSE TO HOLY WAR

Aaron D. Taylor

FOGHORN
PUBLISHERS
"Of Making Many Books There Is No E

TI0434011

Alone With a Jihadist
A Biblical Response to Holy War

ISBN-10: 1-934466-13-1
ISBN-13: 978-1-934466-13-1
Printed in the United States of America
©2009 by Aaron D. Taylor. All Rights Reserved.

Foghorn Publishers
P.O. Box 8286
Manchester, CT 06040-0286
860-216-5622
foghornpublisher@aol.com
www.foghornpublisher.com

Dedication

This book is dedicated to everyone who has loved, supported, and encouraged me over the years as I've traveled the nations preaching the gospel. Without the prayers and financial support of my faithful partners, I would probably be stuck in a dead-end job wishing I were somewhere else. Thank you so much for your sacrifice.

A special thanks to my beautiful wife Rhiannon, who has put up with my endless ramblings, and sleepless nights throughout the writing of this manuscript. Rhiannon, you're a treasure. And to my future children, I pray that you'll read this someday and carry on the legacy of peace through our Lord and Savior Jesus Christ.

Dear Isabelle,

I hope you enjoy the book.

Peace,

Aaron

Endorsements

Aaron Taylor is one of the best students I have ever taught. His new book, *Alone with a Jihadist* is a profound story of how he has moved from the Augustinian idea of a "just war" to the proactive pacifism of early Christianity. This book is must reading for everyone who is concerned about reaching the Islamic world for Jesus. Whether you agree with Aaron's conclusions or not, you will be a wiser and more insightful person after reading this book.

Dr. Eddie L. Hyatt
Author of *2000 Years of Charismatic Christianity*

Aaron D. Taylor has written a compelling challenge to the growing militarism in American fundamentalist Christianity. While remaining true to his Pentecostal/Charismatic roots, Taylor delivers a timely warning to evangelicals worldwide about the dangers of combining religion with nationalism. For those interested in a truly Christian response to the threat of global terrorism, this is the book to read!

Stephen Sizer
Author of *Zion's Christian Soldiers?*

Foreword

Aaron D. Taylor's work, *Alone with a Jihadist* is a God-glorifying prophetic testimony and invitation to faithfulness, and I rejoice that we can together participate in the Spirit's work of renewal and revolution. When I first found nonviolence in my Pentecostal heritage I felt that I had been betrayed because I had been raised to love Jesus, but I never knew that when Jesus said, "love your enemies," he also meant "don't kill them!" An identity shattering and character-transforming journey followed and until now, I am still working out what it means to truly follow Jesus.

For our journeys toward peacemaking, whether as Pentecostal/Charismatic Christians or not, are often difficult and the challenges are clearly seen and felt in Aaron's book. Jesus is supposed to matter for Christians, and *Alone with a Jihadist* reminds me of the way many early Pentecostals explained their peace witness even as many around them rushed to war. That first generation Pentecostal expression of pacifism was largely lost in the United States of America. This book represents a part of a revival on the importance of nonviolence in Christianity.

In this foreword, I will share some early Pentecostal testimonies so that Aaron's voice and life will not be viewed as simply one who is crying out in the wilderness all alone. He is flowing in a prophetic tradition that includes personalities of antiquity such as, Amos, Jeremiah, and Jesus as well as early Pentecostals like William Seymour, C.H. Mason, Arthur Sydney Booth-Clibborn, and Frank Bartleman.

First Generation Pentecostal Critiques of Nationalism

The majority of early Pentecostals believed that "Christians" fundamental allegiance should never be lodged with the state since the state was an earthly fabrication. Like the Tower of Babel, the state signaled human presumption at best, the enthronement of godlessness, immorality, greed, and violence at worst." [1]

The Federal Bureau of Investigation (FBI) charged that Bishop C.H. Mason (1866–1961), founder of the Church of God in Christ, "openly advised against registration [for the draft] and made treasonable and seditious remarks against the United States government." [2] The FBI believed that Mason could be convicted of treason, obstructing the draft, and giving aid and comfort to the

---

1 Grant Wacker, *Heaven Below* (Cambridge: Harvard, 2001), 217. He employs "state" to represent political and governmental structures, "land" to represent the cultural and emotional symbols associated with place, and "nation" to embrace both.

2 Agent M.M. Schaumburger to Bureau of Investigation, September 24, 1917, Old German case file 144128, Record Group 65, Investigation Case Files of the Bureau of Investigation, National Archives. Cited in Theodore Kornweibel, Jr., "Race and Conscientious Objection in World War I: The Story of the Church of God in Christ," in *Proclaim Peace: Christian Pacifism From Unexpected Quarters*, edited by Theron Schlabach and Richard Hughes (Chicago: University of Illinois Press, 1997), 61.

enemy. Both the FBI and the War Department opened files on Mason and the Church of God in Christ, and Mason interviewed with multiple agents. Although Mason publically professed loyalty to the United States, he would not allow his loyalty to dominate or silence his kingdom citizenship and witness, even in the midst of intense patriotism during World War I.

Frank Bartleman (1871–1936) condemned specific injustices of many nations, from England and America to Germany, Russia, Italy, France, and Japan, declaring that "We speak without fear or favor... We favor no country." [3] His Christian citizenship provided the critical distance needed to call out the sins of all nations. Lest anyone question his lack of loyalty to the government of the United States, he provided his attitude toward national fidelity. "Patriotism has been fanned into a flame. The religious passion has been invoked, and the national gods called upon for defense in each case. What blasphemy!" [4] He continued his tirade against nationalism, defended the disenfranchised, and added a call to repentance, "It is not worthwhile for Christians to wax warm in patriotism over this world's situation... American capitalists, leaders and manufacturers are as deep in the mud as the others... " [5]

Bartleman believed that "there is no righteous nation in the earth today" and blamed "nominal Christianity," the opposite of radical

---

3 Frank Bartleman, "The European War," *The Weekly Evangel*, 10 July 1915, 3.
4 Ibid.
5 Frank Bartleman, "What Will the Harvest Be?" *The Weekly Evangel*, 7 August 1915, 1.

prophetic Pentecostal Christianity, for the disastrous atrocities perpetrated by America. We have killed off about all of our American Indians. What we have not killed outright we have starved... Will not God deal in judgment with such a nation as this? Most assuredly! We have stolen the land from the North American Indians... Our wrong to the black people was avenged in blood. What will the next be? [6]

Stanley Frodsham (1882–1969), editor of *The Pentecostal Evangel* for nearly thirty years, believed that "when one comes into that higher kingdom and becomes a citizen of that 'holy nation' (1 Peter 2:9), the things that pertain to earth should forever lose their hold, even that natural love for the nation where one happened to be born, and loyalty to the new King should swallow up all other loyalties." [7] Some Pentecostals saw the slavery, genocide, and greed of the American experiment quite clearly and attempted to speak prophetically about it. These Pentecostals were not the bishops allied with the kings, using the peasants on the front lines to advance the empire.

Wacker notes that Pentecostals often argued, "the United States did not deserve Christians' allegiance" and that "no state, including the United States, had ever been Christian." [8] They preached that the greatest spiritual evil of the age was "immoderate patriotism"

---

6 Ibid., 2.

7 Stanley H. Frodsham, "Our Heavenly Citizenship," *The Weekly Evangel*, 11 September 1915, 3.

8 Wacker, *Heaven Below*, 218.

that led to "national sectarianism," [9] and that Fourth of July celebrations were wastes of God's money. [10] Pentecostals also bravely questioned democracy, viewing it as a political scheme by which humans could accomplish their prideful goals. They called democracy the political system condemned in Daniel, "rule of the people with God left out," control by "popular passion," and concluded "Democracy will not save the world, Republicanism will not bring the Millennium." [11]

First Generation Pentecostal Critiques of War

"The War Church is a Harlot Church!" [12] So says an early twentieth century Pentecostal preacher. This statement offends both the church, which supports war and prostitutes. It echoes the Hebrew Scriptures' comparisons of the unfaithful people of God with people who sell their bodies for sex, and his critique declared that the people of God had sold out, had prostituted themselves, when they supported the European War in 1917 and 1918. The contemporary American church can learn from this first generation prophetic peace witness, but perhaps without the harsh language.

J. W. Welch (1858–1939), the General Superintendent of the Assemblies of God during World War I (1915–20, 1923–25), expressed their official opinion regarding military service. He

---

9 H. Musgrave Reade, in *Trust*, November 1917, 13. Quoted in Wacker, 218.

10 Levi Lupton, in *News Acts*, July 4, 1906, 8. Quoted in Wacker, 219.

11 Wacker, *Heaven Below*, 219.

12 Frank Bartleman, "War and the Christian" (n.p: by the author, circa 1922).

claimed they were trying "to interpret as clearly as possible what the Scriptures teach upon the subject, as we have from the beginning declared the Bible to be our only rule of faith and practice." [13] He told the constituency that they should be willing to serve in any capacity that did not require killing and that he himself was appalled at the idea of Pentecostal men bearing arms.

From the very beginning, the movement has been characterized by Quaker principles. The laws of the Kingdom, laid down by our elder brother, Jesus Christ, in His Sermon on the Mount, have been *unqualifiedly* adopted, consequently the movement has found itself opposed to the spilling of the blood of any man, or of offering resistance to *any* aggression. *Every* branch of the movement, whether in the United States, Canada, Great Britain or Germany, has held to this principle. [14]

Frank Bartleman voiced the concerns of the marginalized in society and condemned war in no uncertain terms while proclaiming that only hypocrites pray for peace while helping the war to continue. The nation, the voters, the church members, could stop this if they would insist upon it... [but] we are willing to receive these millions of blood money. We had better pluck out the stars from our flag and instate dollar marks in their place. [15]

---

13 J. W. Welch, "An Explanation," *The Weekly Evangel*, 19 May 1917, 8.

14 "The Pentecostal Movement and the Conscription Law," *The Weekly Evangel*, 4 August 1917, 6.

15 Frank Bartleman, "The European War," *The Weekly Evangel*, 10 July 1915, 3.

Samuel Booth-Clibborn (b. 1867) employed a Scripture-laden approach to show the absolute nature of Christian nonviolence. He separated Christians from "Pacifists" who used mere politics and "Socialists" who, although their "zeal for peace" was admired, worshipped materialism. [16] In the context of World War I Booth-Clibborn addressed his message to Christians.

Yes, us Christians, who have been preaching this Gospel of LOVE, JOY, and PEACE so loud and so long. Now that it has come to practicing what we preach, now the fiery test will be applied—are we willing to go through for Jesus? Find me in the New Testament where Christ ever sent His followers on such a mission? On the contrary He sent them out to save men—not to butcher them like cattle... No! as far as the Christian is concerned, the "eye for an eye" system has given place to the "Turn to him the other cheek also" of Matthew 5:39–44. [17]

---

16 Samuel H. Booth-Clibborn, "The Christian and War. Is it too Late?," *The Weekly Evangel*, 28 April 1917, 5. "A truly enlightened Christian will have the spiritual perception to see that this so-called 'non-combatant service' is only a part and parcel of the whole machine. Men and women thus employed are every bit as guilty in the Supreme Court of Heaven of the murder of their fellow-men, as are those in the trenches." Samuel H. Booth-Clibborn, *Should A Christian Fight? An Appeal to Christian Young Men of All Nations* (Swengel, PA: Bible Truth Depot, n.d.), 83.

17 Ibid. For another way to interpret the issue of "eye for an eye" and "turn the other cheek" see "If Abraham is our Father" in John Howard Yoder, *The Original Revolution: Essays on Christian Pacifism* (Scottdale: Herald Press, 1998), 91-111

He praised the faithfulness of early Christians and radical movements who did not fight with violence and who did not succumb to patriotism. He wanted Pentecostals to stay true to their prophetic, Spirit empowered, nonviolent origins.

It should be clear from the previous examples of early Pentecostal pacifism and non-nationalism that a usable past does not have to be fabricated; it emerges from a careful examination of the primary sources. Furthermore, I believe that the early Pentecostals, as fallible as they were, identified, adopted, and proclaimed better theology than worse when they took their stand as peace churches. I hope that the revisionism that has perhaps reflected an embarrassment about the early peace witness can be corrected and that a Pentecostal peace with justice witness can continue to emerge and in the power of the Holy Spirit help transform both the world and ourselves in the 21st century and beyond. To Aaron D. Taylor's admirable attempt we now turn.

Paul Alexander, Ph.D.
Founder of Pentecostals & Charismatics for Peace and Justice
Author of *Signs and Wonders: Why Pentecostalism Is the World's Fastest Growing Faith* and *Peace to War: Shifting Allegiances in the Assemblies of God* (The C. Henri Smith Series)

Table of Contents

CHAPTER 1

Alone with a Jihadist

What have I gotten myself into this time? Here I was sitting across the table from Stephen Marshall, the director of a feature length documentary film called Holy Wars, a film examining the role of religion in the post 9/11 clash between the West and Islam. Stephen and I were sitting in an underground café in London discussing what I was about to do the next day. In less than 24 hours, I was about to be stuck in an abandoned warehouse for several hours with a radical jihadist who wanted to destroy me, my country, my religion, and everything else I held dear.

As a 28 year-old evangelist born and raised in Jefferson County Missouri, a rural county outside the suburbs of St. Louis, the idea of representing Western Civilization in an epic debate seemed a bit far-fetched. I imagined what the cultural elite in Europe would think, if they knew a Christian missionary from the Bible Belt was their de facto representative for defending their civilization over and against Islamic civilization. The thought suddenly struck me as humorous. How in the world did I get here?

It all started when I was a young child attending a missionary conference at my charismatic mega-church. As long as I can remember, I've always had a knack for adventure and a zeal for the things of God. When I was between the ages of 8 and 10, my church invited missionaries from all over the world to display exhibits and share about their ministries at an event they called the World Harvest Conference. Seeing the missionaries dressed in exotic costumes and hearing their stories made me want to "abandon it all for the sake of the call" just as they had done. For a young child who rarely traveled, the prospect of spending my life in a far away place and learning another language captured my imagination and gave me a vision for the future. By the time my uncle Charlie took his first trip to Africa, I was hooked. I knew I wanted to be a missionary too.

My first missionary trip was in 1993 to the country of Poland. A missionary from our church named Jack Harris was scheduled to conduct an evangelistic crusade in the town of Wroclaw, so he decided to take a group of select young people from our church's youth group to help advertise the meetings during the day, and most importantly, get a taste of the mission field. For days our team did mimes on the streets and invited people to come to an evangelistic crusade at night. One afternoon as we were all resting in our hotel rooms, I read a book by evangelist Mike Francen called *A Quest for Souls*. Francen was personally trained under the legendary T.L. Osborn and saw many of the same miracles that T.L. and his wife Daisy had seen throughout their 50-years of ministry together. For a 15 year old raised in the charismatic movement, looking at pictures of 100,000 people lifting their hands to receive Jesus as Savior was like an adolescent baseball player looking at a picture of Babe Ruth knocking the ball out of Yankee Stadium. For me, the choice was very simple. How could I stay in America and preach the gospel to those who have already heard when there are millions of people around the world who have never had a chance to hear the gospel once? From that day forward, I decided to dedicate my life to becoming a world evangelist.

As soon as I graduated from high school, I was out the door and ready to change the world. During my formative years, my parents made tremendous financial sacrifices to put my brothers and me through Christian school, so we never really traveled much. But now that I had the freedom to determine my future, I found myself traveling to places far and wide. Places I never in my wildest imagination dreamed I would ever go. Places such as India, China, Tibet, Vietnam, Cambodia, Uganda, Grenada, and Laos. Some of these countries were places where those who decide to follow Jesus often pay a terrible price of suffering and persecution and, yet, the joy on their faces reinforced to me that following Jesus is worth the cost, no matter what the cost may be.

In October of 2000, I met my beautiful wife Rhiannon in Dallas, Texas while we were attending the School of Missions at Christ for the Nations Institute. My wife and I were married on October 6th, 2001, approximately three weeks after 9/11. Shortly after we were married, we decided that we wanted to put our missionary training to use by taking the gospel to those of the Muslim faith. We wanted to minister in a country that has a Muslim majority, but also enjoys religious freedom; so after a year and a half of quiet and peaceful suburban living, we packed our bags and moved to the country of Senegal, located in West Africa.

While in Senegal we labored, we cried, we prayed, and we met a lot of fascinating people along the way. Most of our family and friends thought that we were crazy evangelizing Muslims, especially since this was shortly after 9/11, but the fact is our interaction with Muslims was entirely peaceful. Not once did we come across someone who hated us and wanted us out of the country. Although God allowed us a measure of success in Senegal, sometimes life throws curve balls. After 16 short months of missionary living, my wife and I moved back to the U.S. to help my mother-in-law who eventually died of cancer in March of 2005.

It wasn't long before I was off traveling the world again. This time I found myself traveling to Pakistan—a place largely overrun by radical jihadists sympathetic to the likes of people like Osama bin Laden. Neither my wife nor I wanted to be a prime target for kidnapping or execution, so we decided to concentrate our ministry primarily on the Christian minority, encouraging them in their faith and equipping them with Bibles and other tools for witness and evangelism.

It was shortly after my first trip to Pakistan that I met Stephen Marshall. One day as I was checking my e-mail, I noticed an ad I had previously overlooked in a mass e-mail for missionary mobilizers. The headline read, "Hollywood Production Company looking for a young missionary who travels the world to participate in a feature-length documentary." A few days before I saw the e-mail, I already felt I had a direction from the Lord to begin engaging secular media with the gospel, so when Stephen responded to my reply a few days later, I was pleasantly surprised—and overwhelmed. Representing a Christian perspective to the secular media is a tall order, especially when you don't have any control over the editing process. Almost immediately after I got off the phone with Stephen, I wondered if I'd bitten off more than I can chew.

Unfortunately for me, there was little time for second-guessing. Within a few short weeks, Stephen came to my home to interview me and ask me just about every question under the sun regarding my faith, family, and political views. The last thing I wanted to do was to isolate myself unnecessarily from those outside the conservative evangelical fold, so I tried to be as diplomatic as possible when Stephen asked me questions about 9/11, the Iraq War, free-market capitalism, George Bush, and the Republican Party. Little did I know that the microscopic examination of my faith, on that weekend was only the tip of the iceberg. There was still much, much more to come.

Within a few short months, Stephen traveled with me to Pakistan to observe my preaching and to get a first-hand look at the oppression of Christians in a nation largely populated with radical Muslims. It was during the trip to Pakistan that Stephen began speaking to me about a very outspoken jihadist who lived in

London named Khalid. I had seen Khalid on CNN and knew that he was an Irish convert to Islam who had grown up in a Catholic family. After the trip to Pakistan, I honestly thought my role in the film was over. In my mind, I had behaved like a good Christian and had a rare opportunity to expose the plight of the Pakistani Christians to the world.

Little did I know that a few months later, after delivering a sermon at a Pentecostal church in Brazil, a man would walk up to me and tell me that I was supposed to go to London before the end of the year and that, if I would go, then God would give me a great victory. Taking this as a word from God, I thought that maybe I could go and talk to Khalid, find out how he thinks and see if I could persuade him to accept the way and teachings of Christ. It wasn't long before the producers caught wind of the story and decided to set up a meeting between the two of us for the purpose of capturing the conversation on film.

I don't think words can describe the pressure I felt during the two days of what turned out to be an intense debate with Khalid. Not only did I have to make my case for Christ to Khalid, I also knew that I had to be a faithful representative of Christ to the average non-Christian watching the film, many of whom are already convinced in their minds that those who hold to a fundamental belief in Scripture are destined to drag the world into a premature Apocalypse. To top it off, I knew there were American soldiers in Iraq in harm's way and the last thing I wanted to do was to dishonor their service. The fact that the weather was unusually cold and gloomy, and that we were meeting in an old abandoned warehouse, made the atmosphere tense from the start. When Khalid walked into the room with his fiery eyes, intense gaze, and a grey t-shirt with the words "Soldier of Allah" written on the front, I knew the next few hours were not going to be a picnic.

The meeting didn't quite go as I expected. It took all about two minutes for me to realize there wasn't going to be the Dr. Phil moment I had imagined with me helping Khalid to see that deep down inside there's an inner child waiting to be loved. Within no time, Khalid began venting all of his anger, frustration, and rage against my religion, my country, Western Civilization—and me. In the beginning, I did my utmost to keep the conversation on a theological level. Having lived in a Muslim country and studied the basic tenets of Islam, I knew how to engage Muslims in friendly conversation regarding the merits of Christian belief. Most Muslims I had met up until this point, were surprisingly generous about their view of the Bible and the fate of Christians on judgment day. Khalid, on the other hand, made no apology for his belief that every single Christian who has ever lived is heading straight for hell. The way Khalid raged about Iraq, Afghanistan, George Bush, and Tony Blair, I was sure that, in Khalid's mind, the hottest flames in hell are reserved for those who put them in office.

The most frustrating part for me was the more I tried to shift the conversation to theological matters, the more determined Khalid was to condemn the evils of Western Civilization and, in particular, U.S. foreign policy. After sitting and listening for what seemed like hours, besides the occasional interjection here and there, I finally decided to engage Khalid on one of the primary moral objections to political Islam, and that's the issue of religious freedom. For years I've felt that there's a double standard in the liberal media when it comes to the issue of religious freedom in the Islamic world. I always get annoyed when I read news-magazines or hear cable news commentators herald a country like Malaysia as an Islamic paradise for democracy when I know full well that ethnic Malays who decide to switch their religion from Islam to Christianity (or any other religion for that matter) have historically faced imprisonment, torture, and the threat of execution.

Ready for a good debate, I finally stopped Khalid in mid-sentence and blurted out, "Freedom of religion in Islam is a façade. There is no such thing as freedom of religion in Islam."

Expecting to hear a rebuttal, I was genuinely taken aback when Khalid so nonchalantly replied, "No there's not. We don't believe in freedom and democracy. We believe democracy is just a mani-festation of man-made law."

Freedom and democracy equals man-made law? As an American culturally conditioned to think of the words "freedom" and "democ-racy" as inalienable rights endowed by our Creator, the idea that another human being could consciously reject these values was intriguing to me. The association of democracy with man-made law also had a ring of logic to it. After all, we all know that the U.S. Congress and the British Parliament don't wait for a heavenly finger to write on tablets of stone before passing legislation.

Still trying to keep the conversation on a theological level and with little time to think, I responded, "You see that's the difference, because the Bible says in the New Testament, "The letter kills, but the Spirit gives life" (2 Corinthians 3:6).

Wasting no time, Khalid replied, "Yes, but what does that mean? Nobody knows what that means. Not very clear."

Not very clear? What's not clear about living in freedom from legalistic rules and regulations? I thought perhaps I needed to state it another way.

"If society is going to change, then hearts have to change," I said.

Khalid wasn't buying it, "You still haven't described how you would implement the Bible as a way of life or in government. I'll be honest with you. I'm gonna pin you down. I don't think you can. I don't think you can, because you can't. With the Bible, how would you address the pedophilia, the prostitution, and the homosexuality from a governmental point of view? How would you address that? You're in charge tomorrow all right? You are the president of the United States, how would you address these problems?"

How would I implement the Bible from a governmental point of view? Now that was a good question. In my mind, I could hear the calm reassuring voice of my senior pastor saying something like, "Now, Aaron. Remember that Christianity isn't about trying to regulate society by setting up earthly governments. It's about forgiveness of sins and a right relationship with God."

"That's right, Pastor," I thought to myself, "but that doesn't really answer his question. If I'm going to make the claim that my faith is the right one, certainly I need to show that if everyone, or at least the vast majority of people, embraced my faith, then society would be better off. After all, there are moral implications to living out the gospel, and these implications aren't limited to the private sphere."

In my heart I knew that Khalid's question was far from insignificant. Even though I knew the standard answer that the purpose for Jesus coming to earth was to die on the cross for our sins. Even though I knew that the gospel is about God's love for sinners, not about sinners striving to achieve moral perfection. Even though I knew that the theme of the Bible is grace and redemption, not condemnation and legalism, there was something in Khalid's question that caused my heart to sink. I knew that Khalid's challenge wasn't something I could dismiss lightly.

"First of all, as Christians, we want godly government," I responded. Perhaps it was a lame answer, but it was all I could think of at the moment.

Unfortunately, Khalid didn't have time for introspection. He wanted an answer right then and there.

"What is godly government? I don't understand. What is godly government? How about a punishment system? Let's pin you down. How about a punishment system? For example, what kind of punishment would you have for homosexuality?"

"That's a good question because Jesus said, "He who is without sin let him cast the first stone." Jesus was going more for the heart on that one. Jesus showed that you can have law, but then what's law without mercy?" I replied. Khalid didn't have time for moral philosophy. He wanted an answer.

"So you really don't know what to do about it do you? That's okay. I don't expect you to know because the reason why you don't know is because the answer is not in there. I wouldn't expect you to know. Let me tell you what we do with homosexuals, okay? They are to be taken to the top of a mountain and thrown off and killed. It's capital punishment. For the one who is an adulterer, if they are unmarried, a hundred lashes. If they're married, stoned to death. This is Islamic Sharia. It's comprehensive. I don't expect you to know. I'm not trying to expose you. I'm trying to be honest with you because you are holding a completely corrupted message that doesn't tell you what to do in these situations. So you shouldn't know."

At this point I was thinking *Keep going Khalid. You are really hanging yourself here.* As an evangelical Christian frustrated at how the media so often lumps my people into the same category as radical Islamists by throwing around the word *fundamentalist,* I wanted the potential audience to see what a *real* fundamentalist looks like, so I calmly replied, "You say that homosexuals should be stoned and killed."

"I didn't say that. God says it." Khalid replied in a matter of fact manner.

"I think that's nuts because Jesus said, "He who is without sin among you, let him cast the first stone.""

Khalid took the bait.

"That's why you are going to hellfire and I'm going to Paradise if I die as a Muslim and you die as a disbeliever. In Islam, you have to follow the message of Mohammed. I don't want you to go to hell."

I found it amusing that Khalid didn't want me to go to hell. That was the reason why *I* was there, because I didn't want *him* to go to hell. The problem was that I was cold, jet-lagged, and mild-tempered while Khalid was hot, awake, and ready for a fight. But the last thing I wanted to do was fight. I didn't want the world to see two religious extremists at each other's throats and I *certainly* didn't want this to turn into a stereotypical match of "You're going to hell" "No, *You're* going to hell." So I decided to put one of the principles of Stephen Covey's *Seven Habits of Highly Effective People* into practice. Seek first to understand, then to be under-stood. I decided to listen to what Khalid had to say—and Khalid wasted no time in saying it.

"I believe the Islamic arguments are stronger than the arguments for Christianity. Only because I've studied them both. And when I read the Koran, believe me Aaron, I swear to God, from my heart to your heart. I just read it and, I was a little bit angry at first. At first, I said, how come this was kept away from me? Who kept this away from me for all of my life and let me lead a miserable existence for 34 years without knowing the truth? Let me think that alcohol is okay, let me do whatever I want because of vicarious atonement. One man gets slaughtered on a cross by the Jews and, all of the sudden; everybody can do whatever they want. Pedophiles, homosexuals, do whatever you want. No individual responsibility. No consequences for your actions. That's what your belief hinges on."

One man gets slaughtered on the cross by the Jews and, all of the sudden; everybody can do whatever they want? No individual responsibility? No consequences for your actions? That's what my belief hinges on? I knew that the picture Khalid was painting was a gross distortion of the Christian faith, but at this point, it really didn't matter. Khalid had a preconceived notion in his mind about what I believed and there was little I could do to change his perception. Finally I said:

"You talk a lot about the ideal society, you say that Mohammed is the final prophet, Islam is the true religion because it gives a comprehensive guide to life that's politically and economically sufficient. I would dispute you in saying the Bible doesn't give a comprehensive guide to life. I would dispute you in saying that, because the Bible *does* have a lot to say about government. The Bibles *does* have a lot to say about, not only outward righteousness, but inward righteousness. So, just because you don't see it doesn't mean that I as a Christian can't look in my Bible and see everything that I need to know to live a righteous life."

Khalid's reply was very revealing.

"But, Aaron. I don't need to look at the book. I can look outside the door at your own society. I can see the prostitution. I can see the adultery. I can see the cheating. I can see the moneymakers, the interest, and the society. Every evil, the pedophilia, the homosexuals allowed to run rife. Nothing is addressed. Evil is allowed to run rampant, okay? And you just keep propagating peace and love and all that sort of thing and it's not really good enough. And, as I say, I don't have to look at the book. I just have to look outside the door. I can see a manifestation of everything in there. Everything bad in your society."

The one thing I appreciated about Khalid was that he made it easy for me to summarize his moral arguments. Christianity is evil because Western Civilization is evil. The two are inextricably linked. Now that Khalid was on a role, he decided to shift the conversation to politics. That's when things started to get interesting.

"In the last election, you come from America right? Who did you vote for? Did you vote for anybody?"

A bit caught off guard, I answered, "Well, yes I did, but let me ask you a question."

Khalid cut me off mid sentence.

"It's a simple question. You did vote for somebody? And what do the people that you vote for do? Explain what they do. Look I'm gonna tell you right? I'm gonna tell you what the people you vote for do. They make law and order. They don't make ice cream. In the House of Representatives and the House of Commons here. They make law and order. They decide what's forbidden and they decide what's allowed. This is called man-made law. Now, do you think God wants us to live by His law or man made law? He wants us to live by His comprehensive law and order. He always did. Why do you think Jesus was persecuted? Because He spoke out against the George Bushes and the Tony Blairs of His day. He was called a fundamentalist, terrorist, and an extremist, new laws of terrorism brought in. So He's arrested, tortured. Is this starting to sound familiar? It should to you, because it's what's happening to Muslims today. Whenever a messenger was sent and he changed the whole of society, he was always terrorized, persecuted, and imprisoned. This is a sign of the people that are speaking the truth. And we believe that man-made law is a big disease. So you're saying that you believe in the law of God and you want to be obedient, but yet you're voting for people like George Bush who are mere men."

"Jesus was an Islamic Fundamentalist?" I thought to myself, "Now *that's* one for the loony bin." The Koran was written approximately 600 years *after* the events surrounding the life and ministry of Jesus, which is why no serious historian accepts that Jesus was a Muslim, unless they accept it by blind faith. According to the Koran, Jesus wasn't a friend to sinners, nor did He actually *die* on a wooden cross. In the Koran, Jesus was a Muslim who prayed five times a day facing Mecca, fasted during the month of Ramadan, and made it his aim to implement the Divine Sharia on the whole of society. The problem with this idea is that both the Bible *and history* agree that Jesus was a threat to the religious establishment of His day. Khalid obviously had it backwards, but the fact that he had it backwards underscored something very revealing about the historical Jesus in my mind. The people that Jesus condemned the most were the Pharisees—the ones who ruled over others in the name of God with the power of the State behind them. In a strange way, Khalid's crazy idea served to reinforce the point that he was making. The Jesus of the gospels left us with neither a legal system nor a socio-economic system for creating an ideal society.

Now that Khalid knew he had my attention, he decided to walk me through the finer points of his worldview as a maestro would with an inquisitive pupil.

"Islam is not religion; you probably think Islam is a religion. It's not. It's a pure divine belief. Comprehensive. We had a divine social system, economic system, political system, private system, and a system of what to do when somebody invades your land, what to do when somebody invades your home. We're onto the concept which a lot of people are talking about today, the issue of fighting or jihad in Islam. Jihad in Islam is one of the things that protect the Muslims around the world."

"So jihad is primarily *defensive?*" I thought to myself, "Does that include 9/11?"

Khalid and I had an extensive debate on that one—and a host of other topics. For hours upon hours for two days straight Khalid and I went back and forth on just about every topic imaginable: the prophethood of Muhammad, the crucifixion, the divinity of Jesus, the inspiration of Scripture, Osama bin Laden, Iraq, Afghanistan, the War on Terror, democracy, freedom of religion, the role of women, the persecution of Christians in Muslim lands, the finer points of Sharia law.

In many ways, I felt that I took a beating in my debate with Khalid, though I still walked out of there with my head held high. Rather than feeding the fire-breathing stereotype of a my-way-or-the-highway American evangelist, I decided in the end to make a symbolic attempt at reconciliation. Though Khalid left me with little hope of reconciliation between the West and Islam, I found out later that my presence did have a disarming effect on Khalid—somewhat. Khalid conceded that I wasn't what he expected and, at the very least, he confided to me that I helped him see that American Christians are also concerned about the moral issues he's concerned with and that not every American Christian agrees with U.S. foreign policy. Then I returned home.

For weeks I walked around in a daze. I couldn't get the thought out of my mind that if Khalid and his repeated threats to fight with all means necessary until U.S. troops are removed from Muslim lands. If his ideas represent only 10% of the 1.3 billion Muslims of the world, then we are looking at a problem of global significance. Hearing the rage and frustration of Khalid helped me to see that the anger and frustration of millions of Muslims directed at America and Western Civilization didn't emerge from a vacuum. And how many Jihadists does it take to execute a terrorist attack capable of destabilizing the world order? Only a handful. All I could think of was America is not ready for this. But then another thought struck me.

As I poured myself into watching documentaries, reading scholarly journals online, and scrutinizing the TV news, I realized that something was changing on the inside of me, but I couldn't put my finger on what it was. After a couple of months I realized that something had happened during my debate with Khalid that I never thought would happen. Khalid had presented an authentic challenge to my faith and I knew that if there was to be any victory at all, like the victory that was prophesied, then I would have to get to the bottom of the issue. Khalid's charge was simple. Jesus didn't leave the world with a comprehensive social system, economic system, political system, or any other kind of system to regulate society. At least Muhammad *attempted* to solve the world's problems.

Tell me, preacher man. How would you implement the Bible from a governmental point of view? I poured over the Scriptures for months with this question in mind. Did Jesus really leave us with nothing in terms of how to implement the Scriptures from a governmental point of view? Certainly he left us with something. Or did He? If He did, then we Christians in the West had better find out what it is and get off our lazy derrieres and do something. If He didn't, then why didn't He? If it turns out that He did not, then what are the implications for the War on Terror and the current clash between the West and Islam? After months of pouring over this simple question, I realized that my entire world had been turned upside down.

CHAPTER 2

Sitting in Moses' Seat

Anyone who applies himself to reading the Bible over a lifetime is bound to come up with a favorite verse, a favorite passage, or a favorite book. Allow me to submit to you mine. It's Romans 8:35–39, where the Apostle Paul begins with, "Who shall separate us from the love of Christ?" and ends with: "For I am persuaded that neither death nor life, nor angels nor principalities nor powers, nor things present nor things to come, nor height nor depth, nor any other created thing, shall be able to separate us from the love of God which is in Christ Jesus our Lord." At the time of this writing, I'm not yet 30, but I haven't found anything yet that compares to the unconditional love of Christ, and neither do I expect I ever will. Ask me my favorite book in the Bible and I'll give you a slightly different answer. It's Ecclesiastes hands down.

Maybe it's a generational thing that I find it emotionally gripping when I read about a man who spent his entire life searching for something only to find that in the end, "All is vanity and grasping for the wind" (Ecclesiastes 1:14). In some ways, I think my life over the past year mirrors Solomon's story. No I haven't spent the last year going to wild parties and fooling around with multiple women in the search for pleasure, but I did spend a year of my life searching for something, searching for the answer to the question Khalid posed to me on that fateful day in an old-abandoned warehouse. "Tell me Aaron, how would you implement the Bible from a governmental point of view?" On this question I've spent the past year searching and searching and searching only to find in the end what I suspected all along. The Bible *can't* be implemented from a governmental perspective!

I know that there are *many* who would disagree with me on this. Some say capitalism is God's economic system. Others say its socialism. Scores of books have been written about whether Jesus agrees with the Republicans or with the Democrats. Both parties love to claim Him as one of their own. If a politician wants to win an election, all they have to do is declare their allegiance to Jesus Christ and all of the sudden they're no longer as polarizing as they used to be—at least among the religious crowd.

As much as I love Jesus, focusing on His character made my search for the perfect "Christian" government perplexing. I found that when I matched all the different philosophies of government proposed in the name of Christianity up to the image of Jesus in the gospels, I made an astounding discovery. None of them even came close.

Take for example a very popular movement in the U.S.A. called Christian Reconstructionism. Christian Reconstructionism is a powerful minority movement within the Christian Right that wants to implement the penal codes of the Torah on the whole of society, starting with the preaching of the gospel, but then gradually taking over political and social institutions and conforming them to God's law as revealed in the first five books of the Old Testament. The underlying premise is that the Torah wasn't just for the children of Israel under the Old Covenant; the Torah is God's blueprint for society and should be applied to *all* earthly governments.

As holy and righteous as this ideology sounds, let's look at what a Reconstructed society would look like. The year is 2,100 A.D. and Jack Smith, the patriarchal elder of the Smith Family Clan is skimming over the paperwork from the case load he is about to make a ruling on the next day. In the case of Joe Smith, the nephew who discovered his wife sleeping with another man, Jack Smith knows exactly what to do. According to Leviticus 20:10, the penalty is death. Case number two is also pretty straightforward. John Doe has dragged Katie Smith to court for grabbling his genitals. Jack Smith also knows what to do in this case. Even though Katie's defense is that she did it to protect her husband, the penalty in Deuteronomy 25:11–12 for this case is crystal clear. The law says to cut off Katie's hand without pity. Case number three is a bit trickier. Bob and Sally Smith's teenage son, Joe Smith has been a bit unruly lately. Joe has gone out more than five times in the past month to get wasted with his friends. Since Joe's behavior is a bit of an aberration, it's unclear whether he should be classified as a rebellious youth according to the standards set out in Deuteronomy 21:18–21. The capital punishment case for Joe Smith is still pending.

Khalid's worldview says that all of society's problems would magically disappear if human governments would implement God's law as revealed in the Koran. Ironically, our future friend Jack Smith's worldview isn't much different—except for the fact that it happens to be Moses that Jack seeks to emulate, not Muhammad. The Law of Moses and Sharia are strikingly similar. Both prescribe capital punishment for victimless sex crimes, such as adultery and homosexuality. Both prescribe the chopping off of hands for certain crimes (such as thievery in the Koran and genital grabbing in the Torah). As harsh as the punishments may sound to modern day Westerners, the worldviews of the Islamist and the Christian Reconstructionist shouldn't be dismissed lightly. After all, adultery and fornication wreak havoc on societies and create endless social problems. And what religious minded person wouldn't agree that the breakdown of the family is society's death knell? Why not take care of these problems through implementing God's law? Moses did.

There's only one problem with this idea from a Christian standpoint, and that's the thorny little problem that Jesus never did anything like that. The inconvenient truth about Jesus for those who would like to sit in Moses' seat today is that when Jesus walked the earth, He was a friend to sinners and an enemy to the religious establishment. Jesus never came close to threatening the use of force to control other people's behavior. His primary interests were healing the sick, befriending the outcast, and ticking off the Pharisees. Jesus' disregard for taking on the role of Torah enforcer was also passed onto His followers. When an eccentric Corinthian Christian male was discovered having an incestuous relationship with his mother-in-law (a prime candidate for stoning in Moses' day), the Apostle Paul prescribed excommunication, not capital punishment (I Corinthians 5:13). And even excommunication was temporary. Had the man repented, He would have been accepted back into the fold with open arms (Galatians 6:1–2).

It's not that the Law of Moses is necessarily wicked or evil. In fact, if we judge Moses by the standards of his time, the laws of ancient Israel were…well…progressive. Our 21st century sense of justice might be offended by some of the harsher penalties in the law, but we should understand that our sense of justice is a *Jewish* sense of justice. For example, the idea that a punishment should fit the crime comes directly from Exodus 21:21 which say, "An eye for an eye and a tooth for a tooth." The idea of innocent until proven guilty comes from Deuteronomy 17:16, which says, "Out of the mouths of two to three witnesses shall every word be established." As far as punishment for stealing, Moses didn't cut off people's hands. Instead, the thief had to repay the victim *two to four times* the amount of the stolen item, depending on the item (Exodus 22:1–15). Cutting off the thief's hand may punish the thief, but it doesn't really help the victim.

Israel arguably had the best set of laws under the sun during the Old Testament era and what was the result? The result was prophet after prophet rebuking the people for their idolatry, violence, lust for material possessions, and their oppression of the poor. Khalid and those who follow his version of radical Islam seem to think that theocracy will solve the world's problems. The problem with this view is theocracy was tried once and it turned out to be a big fat failure. If we read the Bible as a narrative, then we have to conclude that theocracy doesn't work. The very things that theocracy was supposed to prevent actually *increased* under theocratic rule. The thorny little problem with the idea that theocracy will solve the world's problems is the simple reality of human nature. Human beings don't like to be told what to do regardless of who's giving the orders. Most human beings who are forced to conform to a strict set of laws will rebel every chance they can get.

Case in point. More people in Iran have converted to Christianity *since* the revolution in 1979 than any other post-Muhammad period of history *combined*. How ironic is it that Iranian Mullahs who take on the role of fashion police to consolidate their power are actually driving people *away* from Islam! One concerned Iranian intellectual put it this way; "These young people may be lost to Islam forever.... They follow the conventions of Islamic dress and custom, because they are required to do so by law, but inside their hearts are hollow and cynical. We are losing an entire generation of unbelievers in our zeal to force conformity." [1]

Exactly! Theocratic rule can force outward conformity, but it can never force inward conformity. Human beings can't be micromanaged and controlled like hamsters. They will always throw a curve

---

1 *Christianity Today*, July 2007, 64

ball in one way or another. I find it ironic that Khalid converted to Islam while spending time in a Saudi Arabian prison for *bootlegging.* Even in holy Saudi Arabia, people found a way to get hammered.

It didn't take very long for me to reject Torah-style theocracy as a viable philosophy for Christian government. Had Joseph carried out what the Torah required him to do, Mary would have been executed on the spot, but Matthew describes Joseph as a just man precisely because he did *not* do what the Torah required (Matthew 1:19). Unlike the children of Israel under the Torah, the Apostle Paul confronted witchcraft and sorcery in his day through preaching the gospel and casting out demons, not by death threats. Even more damaging to the claims of those who believe God has called them to be the moral guardians of society is the annoying little fact that the Apostle Paul could care less about how people *outside* the Church behaved. Paul's sole concern was for those *inside* the Church. Take for example what Paul says in I Corinthians 5:9–13:

"I wrote to you in my epistle not to keep company with sexually immoral people. Yet I certainly did not mean with the sexually immoral people of this world, or with the covetous, or extortioners, or idolaters, since then you would need to go out of the world. But now I have written to you not to keep company with anyone named a brother, who is sexually immoral, or covetous, or an idolater, or a reviler, or a drunkard, or an extortioner-not even to eat with such a person. *For what have I to do with judging those also who are outside?* Do you not judge those who are inside? *But those who are outside God judges.* Therefore 'put away from yourselves the evil person'" (italics emphasis mine).

After a careful reading of the gospels, one of the things that I discovered was that Jesus wasn't interested in interfering with the matters of the State. He wasn't even interested in interpreting the Mosaic Law to settle disputes when people asked Him to.

Take for example the day a man came up to Jesus and said, "Teacher, tell my brother to divide the inheritance with me," (Luke 12:13). If there was ever a time during His earthly ministry where Jesus could have set Himself apart as a legal expert in civil affairs, this was it. Here's a guy who needed help and Jesus certainly would have been familiar with the inheritance laws as laid out in the Torah. But notice what Jesus says,

"Man, who made me a judge or an arbitrator over you?" (Vs 14)

Either Jesus had a sudden memory loss and forgot who He was or He simply wasn't interested in exercising *any* type of earthly power over others. As a late Gen-X Christian born and raised in the charismatic movement, I find this verse even more mystifying because I've always assumed that society would be better off if more Christians would seize the reigns of political power and restore godly values through righteous legislation. After I met Khalid and discovered the end result of an ideology bent on world domination by holy writ, I began to rethink this assumption. I realized that had Jesus wanted to seize the reigns of political power to establish a just society, He certainly could have. After all, who is the one person in history who *could have* used the power of an earthly throne for righteous purposes? But it's precisely at this point where Jesus baffles me the most. Jesus rejected political power not once, not twice, but three different times, and one of the times, it was *Satan* that offered it to Him! (Luke 4:5–8) [2] Why would the New Testament authors want us to know that it was Satan that tempted Jesus to acquire political power? Could it be that the more Christians pursue political power to control other people's behavior, the less we look like Jesus?

I realize I'm treading on sacred ground here, but the suggestion is worth considering. Jesus walked and talked like His sole agenda was to love God and serve people. Instead of ruling with a sword or a gavel, He ruled with a towel. Instead of exercising power *over* people, He exercised power *under* people. Rather than taking on the role of a master, He took on the role of a servant. Jesus washed His disciples feet and taught them to do the same (John 13:1–17). Jesus displayed zero concern for land and buildings. He wasn't interested in overthrowing the Romans, nor did He have any interest in keeping Jerusalem in the hands of Jews, as many of today's "Christian" political activists do. His sole concern was loving people. I wonder what it would look like today if Christians refused to pursue any other agenda but to imitate Jesus? What if our sole earthly agenda was to love people, serve people, and meet their needs?

Think of all the times the multitudes came to Jesus with their sicknesses and their diseases. I imagine there were a few prostitutes, a few adulterers, a few witches in the crowds—not to

---

2 The other two times were after He fed the 5,000 (John 6:5) and the triumphal entry into Jerusalem shortly before His crucifixion (Matthew 21:1–17, Mark 11:1–11, Luke 19:28–44)

mention a few men and women with sexual orientation issues—who came to Him for healing. Did Jesus sit in Moses' seat and take on the role of Inquisitor? Did He make them confess their sins so He could turn them over to the religious courts? How about those annoying Canaanites living in God's holy land that the Jews were supposed to wipe out under Joshua? How did Jesus treat them? Did He care who they were or where they came from? Hardly. He healed *all* who came to Him. (Matthew 8:16, 12:15, Luke 6:19)

Not only was Jesus *not* interested in exercising earthly power over others, He also went out of His way to *befriend* those who were polluting the society of His day. One of the things I find most fascinating about Jesus is His utter disregard for His reputation in reaching out to the people the religious establishment of His day rejected. Jesus was called a glutton and a winebibber because He hung out with tax collectors and sinners (Matthew 11:19, Luke 7:34). Unlike the "Moral Majority" which at one time made it their aim to deny housing to gay people, Jesus never seemed interested in using political power to push sinners to the fringes of society. All He seemed to be interested in was loving people and meeting their needs, regardless of who they were or what they needed. If a wedding party ran out of wine, He turned the water into wine (John 2:1–12). If an idol-worshiping pagan needed healing for her demonized daughter, He healed her (Matthew 15:22–28). If a two-timing tramp needed living water to quench her spiritual thirst, He offered it—no questions asked (John 4:1–26). Given the political and religious expectations of the Jews during the time of Jesus, the last thing I would want to be if I were around during this time would be the P.R. guy trying to promote His ministry!

If we narrow the Kingdom of God to the parameters of that which looks, thinks, and acts like Jesus, then we have to conclude that God's kingdom has nothing to do with exercising power or authority over others—in any way, shape, or form. Jesus' disciples may have wanted to sit on earthly thrones, but Jesus didn't. When His disciples asked Him who would be the greatest in the Kingdom of Heaven, they were thinking of political power. I imagine they were sorely disappointed when Jesus called a little child, set him in the midst of them and said,

"Assuredly, I say to you, unless you are converted and become as little children, you will by no means enter the kingdom of heaven. Therefore, whoever humbles himself as this little child is the greatest in the kingdom of heaven" (Matthew 18:3–4).

Why did Jesus choose a child as an example of the nature of God's Kingdom? It wasn't because children are cute and cuddly. It's because children were at the bottom of the social ladder. In a society oppressed by a foreign occupation, a society where people struggled day after day just to survive, children were considered useless. They were the least powerful people He could think of. By using a child as an example, Jesus was contrasting His idea of God's kingdom with His disciples' understanding of God's kingdom. The disciples wanted to exercise power *over* others while Jesus wanted to come under people and serve them as a self-sacrificing nobody.

Like most of us, Jesus' disciples were slow learners, because two of His disciples asked the same question again. Only this time, they sent their mother to ask Him who would have the most power and prestige in Christ's earthly New World Order. Jesus again corrected them by saying,

"You know that the rulers of the Gentiles lord it over them, and *those who are great exercise authority over them. Yet it shall not be so among you,* but whoever desires to be great among you, let him be your servant. And whoever desires to be first among you, let him be your slave" (Matthew 20:26–27) (italics emphasis mine).

Notice what Jesus said about political power. He said *it shall not be so among you.* Jesus made it clear that His kingdom isn't about who's the boss, but who's the servant (Or rather, who's the *slave*). The Kingdom of God that Jesus came to bring to the world is an upside down kingdom because it rejects what the world esteems and esteems what the world rejects. The world may esteem the powerful, but Jesus esteems the powerless.

Unless we view the Kingdom of God as a conscious rejection of political power over and against the backdrop of Rome, which deified political power, much of what Jesus taught about the gospel of the kingdom doesn't make much sense. Even the Christmas story doesn't make much sense unless we contrast the baby King Jesus lying in a manger, born to impoverished parents, with King Augustus sitting on the imperial throne wielding the power of the sword. Notice how Mary the mother of Jesus esteemed the powerless over the powerful in the Magnificent:

"He has shown strength with His arm; He has scattered the proud in the imagination of their hearts. He has put down the mighty from their thrones, and exalted the lowly. He has filled the hungry with good things, and the rich He has sent away empty" (Luke 1:51–53).

Notice how Mary exalted the poor over the prince, the lowly over the powerful, the meek over the mighty. Mary knew that God's value system is different from the world's value system. Mary seems to have passed this upside down power preference along to her children because if we read James, the brother of Jesus carefully, we can see the same contrast between the kingdom of the powerful and the kingdom of the lowly. What else could James have meant when He wrote, "Has God not chosen the poor of this world to be rich in faith and heirs of the Kingdom which He promised to those who love Him?" (James 2:5). Unless we view "the Kingdom" that James is referring to as a value system which esteems the poor versus the Kingdom of Rome which esteemed the powerful, James' usage of the word "Kingdom" makes little sense.

After centuries of foreign occupation, the Jewish world was looking for a charismatic muscle man to expel the Romans and restore the Jewish throne to its former glory. They were looking for someone to rid the holy land from the pagan Roman culture breathing down their necks—someone to establish God's kingdom once and for all. Is it any wonder that they were taken aback when the heir to Solomon's throne turned out to be the son of a carpenter who associated with the poor and the outcast, mocking imperial power by riding into town on the back of an ass while the people tried to forcibly crown Him king?

Fast-forward 2,000 years and little has changed. The world is still looking to political saviors to solve its problems and, like a sick joke; the politicians keep letting us down again and again. We worship Jesus with our lips and yet if a modern Pontius Pilate gave the average evangelical Christian in America a choice between Jesus, the enemy loving foot-washer, and Barabbas, the holy warrior, I wonder which one we'd choose?

CHAPTER 3

The Kingdom of God vs the Kingdom of the Sword

As soon as I realized that Khalid was right about the fact that Jesus never attempted to leave the world with a governmental system to solve its problems, my head began to spin. I began to reflect on the fact that I live in a country founded on a system that our founders believed would bring about a New World Order for mankind. I began to think about all the "isms" associated with American-style democracy; Neo-liberalism, Globalism, and Free-market capitalism. All of these "isms" are staples of the U.S. economic diet that both democrats and republicans seem to agree that is what the world needs. Then I began to reflect on the carnage in Iraq following the aftermath of the U.S. invasion that was supposed to bring U.S. style "freedom" to the Iraqis. By the time I allowed myself to reflect on Katrina, the devastating hurricane that crashed down on New Orleans, exposing the plight of an obvious underclass, I wondered if our American "ism" is all that it's cracked up to be—and whether it should be imposed on others at the barrel of a gun. Once I realized that my world-view was going through a drastic overhaul, I turned to the last place a Bible-belt evangelical raised in the charismatic movement would ever be expected to turn to find answers—the Pope.

One day, as I was browsing through the bookshelf at a Barnes & Noble Bookstore, I came across a book by Pope Benedict XVI called *Jesus of Nazareth.* I'd heard that the current Pope is known for his theological brilliance, so I decided to pick his brain for a few minutes—and what I found floored me. Take for example what the Pope has to say about earthly kingdoms and those who believe they have the answers to solve the world's problems.

"Earthly kingdoms remain earthly human kingdoms, and anyone who claims to be able to establish the perfect world is the willing dupe of Satan and plays the world right into his hands." [3]

Does *anyone* include politicians or is it *especially* politicians the Pope has in mind? What happens when a politician or would-be revolutionary believes the system reflected in his earthly kingdom, whether it's democracy, socialism, populism, or any other "ism" out there—is the hope for mankind? According to the Pope, that man is a willing dupe of Satan.

---

3 *Jesus of Nazareth* (Doubleday, 2007), 44

Here's another quote that jumped off the page.

"The temptation to use power to secure the faith has arisen again and again in varied forms throughout the centuries, and again and again faith has risked being suffocated in the embrace of power. The struggle for freedom of the Church, the struggle to avoid identifying Jesus' Kingdom with any political structure, is one that has to be fought century after century. For the fusion of faith and political power always comes at a price: faith becomes a servant of power and must bend to its criteria." [4]

How ironic is it that these words are coming from *the Pope?* Given the history of wars, witch-hunts, torture, and cruelty associated with the Catholic Church, is it possible that the leader of the Catholic Church is more advanced than the average Protestant thinker when it comes to the relationship between God's kingdom and worldly kingdoms? The Pope is *not* simply saying that the Church as an institution should never resort to the use of force to spread the Christian faith, nor is He simply saying that religious freedom is a moral non-negotiable in Christianity. The Pope is saying something far more profound. The Pope is saying that those who identify God with an earthly kingdom or political structure play the world into the Devil's hands. In a world where heads of States, rebels, and military generals alike are fond of invoking God to bless their particular projections of earthly power, the Pope is saying that if you want to advance a

---

4 ibid

political agenda, be it through war or the ballot box, please don't stick God's name on it. An astounding piece of wisdom, but where did the Pope get this idea?

The answer is he got it from the gospels. Both Matthew and Luke record an incident in which Satan brought Jesus up to a high mountain, showed Him all the kingdoms of the world in a moment's time and tempted Him by saying, "All this authority I will give You, and their glory; for this has been delivered to me, and I give it to whoever I wish. Therefore if you will worship before me, all will be Yours" (Luke 4:6–7).

It doesn't take a lifetime in Sunday school to predict that Jesus would refuse to bow His knee to Satan, but the puzzling part about this incident is that Jesus didn't dispute Satan's claim. Satan claimed to have authority over all the kingdoms of the earth and that he could give their authority to whomever he wishes, and Jesus didn't bother to correct him! Was Satan telling the truth or was Jesus being polite?

The answer to this question is far from insignificant, because if Satan really does have authority over all the kingdoms of this world, the implications for how Christians relate to earthly governments are vast. If the Scriptures teach that every human government, no matter how good or wonderful it claims to be, is under the dominion of Satan, then what does that say for how a Christian relates to whatever government he or she finds herself living under? Should Christians pledge allegiance to the State, commit to fight for the State, or have any part in running the State when the State is merely one of the many kingdoms of this world under the dominion of Satan?

Christians may be surprised to discover that the rest of the Bible seems to confirm that Satan wasn't exaggerating when he claimed to have authority over all the kingdoms of this world. In the gospel of John, Jesus referred to Satan as the "ruler" of this world three different times (John 12:31, 14:30, 16:11). The word "ruler" that Jesus used is *arche* in the Greek, which referred to the highest ruling authority in any particular region governed by the Roman Empire. The Apostle Paul referred to Satan as "the god of this age" and "the principality and power of the air" (2 Corinthians 4:4 and Ephesians 2:2). The Apostle John in his epistle to the early Church went so far as to write, "The *whole world* lies under the sway of the wicked one" (I John 5:9) (italics emphasis mine).

Ever since the time of Constantine, Christians on the whole have legitimized whatever earthly power structures they've found themselves living under, whether it's monarchy, capitalism, socialism, as if their system of government was God's hand picked "ism" for the world. Not so with the early Christians. When the early Christians got together, they recited prayers harking back to the Book of Psalms. Prayers like:

"Why did the nations rage, And the people plot vain things? The kings of the earth took their stand, and the rulers were gathered together against the Lord and against His Christ." (Psalms 2:1–2, Acts 4:25–26).

Notice the subversive tone in I Corinthians 2:6 where Paul spoke of "the rulers of this age, who are coming to nothing." In light of what the early Christians prayed in the Book of Acts, what else could Paul have meant by "the rulers of this age" other than the Satanic Roman Empire that crucified the Lord Jesus Christ? Think about what the Roman authorities would have thought if they had read Paul's letter. Is it any wonder that the Empire eventually chopped off his head?

Just to be clear, this doesn't mean that all rulers are necessarily evil, some are God-fearing men and women who sincerely want to do right, nor does it mean that God in his sovereignty doesn't use earthly governments to accomplish as much good as possible in a fallen world (Romans 13:1–4). But what are the implications of the fact that the Bible teaches that the world's power-through-the -sword system is under the dominion of Satan? Throughout history, the vast majority of human beings have trusted and relied on the power of this system (aka the State) to secure their lives and their property and to maintain law and order. This is what's called the social contract, and every human government operates from this premise. Human beings bestow power on other human beings to keep them safe. The system seems inevitable to most, but when we look at the narrative of Scripture in its totality, it seems that God has been trying to steer humanity to the conclusion that when human beings are given power over others, they tend to use it in sinful ways.

Think about when the children of Israel requested a king to rule over them. If the centralization of power were what God had in mind to keep human beings from destroying each other, then you would think that God would have been happy with the Israelites for choosing a king. But was God happy with the Israelites for requesting a king to rule over them? No He wasn't. God saw the Israelite's request for a king as a sign of *rejecting* His authority over their lives. Notice what God told the Israelites what would happen if they chose a king to rule over them. In I Samuel 8:11–17, God gave an exhaustive list of what a king would do, like appointing their sons for chariots, appointing captains over thousands and captains over fifties, appointing some to make weapons of war and equipment for chariots, taking a tenth of the people's grain and giving them to his officers and servants—eerily similar to a modern military industrial complex!

God doesn't seem too happy with the arrangement of human beings handing power to other human beings to collect taxes, build armies, and wage wars, but that's what the Israelites wanted, and that's what the vast majority of human beings still want today. Human beings crave for a sense of purpose and belonging, a way to divide the world between us versus them and the State provides the perfect vehicle to satisfy this craving. Throughout history, millions have marched to war, seizing other people's properties; killing people they don't know, fattening the pockets of the ones who sent them—all for the love of the State. And to add insult to injury, the rulers of the nations always believe they're worthy of such single-minded devotion. That's why God laughs at them (Psalms 2:4).

In God's view, "All nations before Him are as nothing, and they are counted by Him less than nothing and worthless." (Isaiah 40:17) As much as people like to pride themselves in whatever nation they find themselves living under, Christians know that God counts every nation as less than nothing and worthless. Christians are supposed to know that Satan is the deceiver of the nations (Revelation 20:3) and that every nation, no matter how good and righteous she claims to be, is deceived by the whore of Babylon's sorcery (Revelation 18:23). All nations advance their self-interests by the power of the sword. No matter how much one nation claims to be more righteous, more holy, than all the other nations, Kingdom of God citizens know better. All nations are a mixture of good and evil and are under the dominion of Satan, even though some versions of earthly kingdoms are better than others.

A careful study of the New Testament reveals there are two types of kingdoms available to mankind—and only two. The Kingdom of God always looks like Jesus and operates from the basis of power through redemptive love and the kingdoms of this world operate from the basis of power-through-the-sword. The Kingdom of God always comes under people to serve them. The kingdoms of this world always rule over people to subdue them. The heavenly King Jesus, the one who suffers and bleeds for His enemies, rules the Kingdom of God. Earthly kings who crush their enemies rule the kingdoms of this world. The two types of kingdoms will always be at odds with each other and only in the end will there be one kingdom left standing.

Though it may seem like earthly kingdoms will last forever, the reality is only God's kingdom is an everlasting kingdom—and God's kingdom is a non-violent kingdom. Two thousand years ago the son of a Jewish carpenter stood before the might of the Roman Empire in the person of Pontius Pilate. Pilate, knowing that a claim to royalty meant a possible insurrection against Caesar, wanted a point blank answer to the question of whether Jesus was the King of the Jews. Jesus, in His usual abstract style, lifted the conversation to a higher plane with a reply destined to become a watershed for human history:

"My Kingdom is not of this world. If My kingdom were of this world, My servants would fight, so that I should be delivered to the Jews, but now my Kingdom is not from here" (John 18:36).

In one simple statement, Jesus laid the foundation for a radically new type of kingdom that is altogether otherworldly. Rather than Caesar-style power through the sword, tit-for-tat retribution, Jesus declared that His kingdom would operate from an entirely different plane altogether. It's crucial to understand that Jesus was *not* simply telling Pilate, "My people don't spread my message through force." Neither was Jesus talking about the Church as an institution raising armies and advocating holy wars. What Pilate would have understood Jesus to be saying was, "I know you may think I'm a rebel because I call myself a King, but you don't have to worry about me fomenting a rebellion against Caesar's puny little empire. Because what distinguishes *My* Kingdom from *Caesar's* kingdom, is, in my Kingdom, my servants don't fight."

Jesus knew that Pilate only operated from one plane of reality, and that's the reality of peace through strength, stability through force. That was the prevailing mindset of the Roman Empire, and Jesus understood the Roman mindset perfectly well. That's why Jesus was surprisingly generous to Pilate when Pilate asked Him, "Do you not know that I have power to crucify You, and power to release You?" (John 19:10) Instead of rebuking Pilate for his pride, Jesus replied by saying, "You could have no power at all against Me unless it had been given you from above. Therefore the one who delivered Me to you has the greater sin" (Vs 11).

Jesus knew that Pilate was operating exclusively from a kingdom of this world perspective, which relies on power through the sword to maintain law and order, keep people in submission, and prevent political messiahs from overthrowing the ruling powers. All earthly governments operate from this premise—even democratic ones. This is why Jesus was more gracious to Pilate than He was to the religious leaders who turned Him over to Pilate. Jesus knew that Pilate was only doing what Pilate had to do because the power-through-the-sword system inherent in *every* kingdom of this world left him with little other choice. When Jesus said, "My Kingdom is not of this world" He was telling Pilate there's an alternative system available that's entirely otherworldly, a new type of kingdom that operates on the principle of non-violent redemptive love, a kingdom in which the citizens of the kingdom don't fight.

Until we understand that the Kingdom of God stands in direct opposition to the power-through-the-sword system inherent in the kingdoms of this world, much of our understanding of the New

Testament will be shallow at best, including our understanding of the gospel. When Jesus and the Apostles preached "the gospel", it was primarily the gospel *of the kingdom* that they preached, but what does the *of the kingdom* part mean if it *doesn't* mean a kingdom that stands in direct opposition to the value system of the only other kingdom the early followers of Jesus would have known at the time—the kingdom of Rome.

The Roman Empire claimed to be the panacea of the world. If people would simply pledge their allegiance to lord Caesar and drink from the fountain of Rome's economic and military might, the world would be a peaceful place—hence the term *Pax Romana* (a term eerily similar to the neoconservative term *Pax Americana* I might add) When the early Christians preached the gospel of the Kingdom and confessed Jesus Christ as Lord, they were telling their fellow Roman citizens there's a new Kingdom in town and it plays by a different set of rules. Inasmuch as the Kingdom of Rome relies on the sword to achieve peace and stability in a chaotic world, the Kingdom of God relies on turning the other cheek, not repaying evil for evil, refusing to take vengeance, and loving one's enemies. (Matthew 5:43–48, Romans 12:14–21). The subversive element of the early church was that the early Christians preached the Kingdom of God as the only Kingdom that followers of Jesus owe their allegiance.

Consider what the Apostle Paul referred to Jesus in his letter to Timothy:

"I urge you in the sight of God who gives life to all things, and before Christ Jesus who witnessed the good confession before

Pontius Pilate, that you keep this commandment without spot, blameless until our Lord Jesus Christ's appearing, which He will manifest in His own time, he who is the blessed and *only* Potentate, the King of Kings and Lord of lords," (I Timothy 6:13–14) (italics emphasis mine).

Notice that the Apostle Paul refers to a confession that Jesus witnessed before Pilate, a confession that Timothy also made in the presence of many witnesses (Vs 12). I've always found this passage puzzling because what confession could both Jesus have made before Pilate *and* Timothy could have made in the presence of many witnesses? We know that the unifying confession for the early Church was "Jesus Christ is Lord" (Romans 10:9–10), so it's reasonable to assume that the confession of Christ's lordship is what Paul is referring to as Timothy's confession of faith, but what about the confession of faith that *Jesus* made? What was Jesus' confession before Pilate that Christians are called to imitate?

I believe the answer is none other than the statement that stands out the most in Jesus' dialogue with Pilate: "My Kingdom is not of this world." Paul was reminding Timothy that when He publicly made the confession "Jesus Christ is Lord", he was identifying Himself as a citizen of a kingdom that is not of this world, a kingdom that operates from a different set of rules than worldly kingdoms. Paul wanted Timothy to remember that when he publicly confessed, "Jesus Christ is Lord", he was also saying, "Caesar is not Lord." When the early Christians confessed Jesus Christ as Lord, they understood that they were professing their allegiance to an otherworldly kingdom and renouncing their allegiance to every other kingdom.

Notice that the Apostle Paul refers to Jesus as the *only* Potentate, a word denoting kingly authority. We know what this meant for Timothy, but what does it mean for Christians today? To put it simply, it means that George Bush may think he's a Potentate, but he's really not. It means that Bill Clinton, John McCain, Barak Obama, General Musharraf, and Vladimir Putin all may think they're Potentates, but they're really not. There's *only one* rightful Potentate. There's only *one rightful* King in this world and that's King Jesus. Kingdom of God citizens owe their allegiance and their obedience to King Jesus and nobody else. Uncle Sam may think he's the rightful authority over our lives, but he's not. Jesus is.

Readers may ask, if Jesus is the *only* authority in a Christian's life, the *only* Potentate, the only King, what are the implications for the relationship between a Christian and the State? The only logical conclusion I can come to is *a Christian is free from the state!* Yes, we obey the laws of the land, but only because *God* wants us to, not because a Christian owes the State anything. And the reason why God wants Christians to be good citizens and obey the laws of the land is because police officers, Prime Ministers, legislative officials, and military personnel are people too, and God would rather have us love them than offend them.

Consider what the Apostle Peter says in I Peter 2:15–17:

"For this is the will of God, that by doing good you may put to silence the ignorance of foolish men—*as free*, yet not using liberty as a cloak for vice, but as bondservants of God. Honor all people. Love the brotherhood. Fear God. Honor the King" (italics emphasis mine).

Notice the words *as free*. Christians are free from any and all obligations to the State, so why does God want us to submit to earthly rulers? The answer is so that by doing good we can put to silence the ignorance of foolish men, the same foolish men that believe the ruler/subject relationship is the only way human beings can relate to each other. As Christians we are free from the State, but we obey lest we offend.

Where did Peter get the idea that followers of Jesus are free from the State? The answer is He got it from Jesus. When the religious leaders asked Peter if his teacher paid the Temple tax, Jesus gave an answer Peter probably wasn't expecting.

"What do you think, Simon? From whom do the kings of the earth take customs or taxes, from their sons or from strangers?" Jesus asked Peter.

"From strangers," Peter replied.

"Then the sons are free," said Jesus.

Had Jesus stopped there, one could easily surmise that followers of Jesus aren't obligated *at all* to pay taxes to earthly kings, and that would be partially correct. Christians are *not* obligated to pay taxes to earthly kings in a manner that suggests earthly kings have any rightful claim over our lives. Only Jesus has the rightful claim over the life of a Christian. In the end, earthly rulers still get their coins not because they're anything special, but because Jesus would rather have His followers loving earthly rulers than offending them. Jesus went on to tell Peter, "Nevertheless, lest we offend them," and then proceeded with paying the tax by pulling the coin out of a fish's mouth.

The Apostle Paul followed the same line of reasoning when he wrote to the Roman Christians of his day, "Owe no man anything except to love one another, (Romans 13:8). As a young Christian aspiring financial independence, I've heard hundreds of self-help gurus use this verse to talk about getting out of debt. As much as I've been inspired (and frustrated) by this interpretation, Paul isn't talking about debt in this passage. When Paul says, "Owe no man anything," He's talking about paying taxes, customs, fear, and honor to earthly rulers (Vs 7). Paul is telling his disciples the reason why Kingdom of God citizens submit to earthly rulers is because God doesn't want His people owing earthly rulers anything except to love them.

The important point to note here is that Romans 13:8 comes directly after the famous passage where Paul seems to legitimize Christians wielding the power of the sword. Historically, Christians have used the first four verses of Romans 13 to tiptoe around the more difficult teachings of Jesus, such as loving your enemies, turning the other cheek, praying for those who perse-cute you, and doing good to those who hate you, as if they don't apply when it comes to a Christian's participation in state affairs.

The common interpretation goes something like this. Christians must obey the teachings of Jesus when it comes to matters of *personal* interest, such as turning the other cheek and not taking *personal* vengeance on others, but when it comes to a Christian participating in State sanctioned vengeance, it's no holds barred! God has ordained the government/military as His instrument to execute wrath on evil-doers, so when a Christian participates in state-sanctioned violence, he or she has God's blessing.

On the surface, the first four verses of Romans 13 seem like a slam- dunk for those who say that Christians are free to wield the power of the sword either as a political ruler or a soldier in a war deemed to be a just cause. Paul says, "the authorities that exist are appointed by God" (Vs 1), "whoever resists the authority resists the ordinance of God" (Vs 2), "rulers are not a terror to good works but to evil" (Vs 3) and tops it off with the clincher:

"For he is God's minister to you for good. But if you do evil, be afraid; for he does not bear the sword in vain; for he is God's minister, an avenger to execute wrath on him who practices evil," (Vs 4).

The Apostle says that the rulers of this world don't bear the sword in vain; therefore a Christian can wield the power of the sword as long as a legitimate authority sanctions it. The logic seems perfectly sound…that is…until you read the verses in context and discover that Paul wasn't writing to *the government* of his day; He was writing to *Christians*, and Paul's underlying assumption is that Christians are the ones being governed, not the ones doing the governing. It's true that Paul calls earthly rulers God's servants, but *Nebuchadnezzar* was also God's servant, and we know that God didn't approve of *his* actions (Jeremiah 25:9, 43:10, Isaiah 13, 14). All we can really know from this passage is that Christians are supposed to be *subject* to earthly rulers and even *that* is only because Christians aren't supposed to owe earthly rulers anything but to love them (Vs 8). For Kingdom of God citizens, Jesus is still the *only* Potentate, and the one thing that Jesus said distinguishes His kingdom from all other kingdoms is that His servants don't fight.

When it comes to how Kingdom of God citizens are supposed to behave, the Apostle Paul makes it very clear in the verses *directly preceding* Romans chapter 13. In these verses, Paul sounds a lot more like Jesus when he says things like, "Bless those who persecute you, Bless and do not curse," (Vs 14), "Repay no one evil for evil," (Vs 17) and then tops it off with:

"Beloved, do not avenge yourselves, but rather give place to wrath; for it is written, 'Vengeance is mine, I will repay,' says the Lord. Therefore 'If your enemy is hungry, feed him; If he is thirsty, give him a drink; For in so doing you will heap coals of fire on his head.' Do not be overcome by evil, but overcome evil with good.'" (Vs 19–21).

While it's true that the Apostle grants the State the right to bear the sword, it doesn't necessarily follow from this passage that *a Christian* has the right to bear the sword in the name of the State, so *the least* that we can say is the Apostle is silent on this issue. But when we factor in the fact that God wasn't too thrilled with the Israelites assigning themselves a king to collect taxes and wage wars, that all earthly governments are under the dominion of Satan, that Jesus is the *only* Potentate, and the one thing that distinguishes the Kingdom of God from the Kingdoms of this world is that servants in the Kingdom of God don't fight, the case for a Christian participating in State sanctioned violence is no longer a slam dunk. More like a long shot. And this doesn't include what Jesus told Peter when Peter took it upon himself to chop off a Roman soldier's ear to prevent Jesus from arrest, "Put your sword in it's place, for all who take the sword will perish by the sword," (Matthew 26:52).

I realize that what I've written so far brings up a lot of questions. Should Christians oppose *all* wars? Can Christians vote? Can a Christian run for political office or serve as a police officer? Can a Christian serve in military combat, or in the military at all? How should Christians relate to police officers, political rulers, and soldiers in the military? With the exception of the last question (which is easy because the Apostles are in unanimous agreement that Christians are supposed to honor and respect those in authority) none of these questions have easy answers. The very least we can say at this point is that an action is not legitimate simply because *the State* says it's legitimate and that the Kingdom of God can never be associated with a version of a kingdom of this world, even if it's a better version than others. As we'll see in the next chapter, when Christians forget this, things can get ugly.

CHAPTER 4

Is Democracy the New Crusade?

S hortly after I returned home from London, I was at a revival
meeting in one of the most prominent mega-churches in
Missouri. Like many meetings I had been to in the past, the
atmosphere was charged with excitement and warmth. There was
the usual period of ecstatic praise and worship along with an
attractive female singing a special on the joys of knowing Christ.
As the guest preacher came to the pulpit, I could feel a sense of
awe permeate the sanctuary of 3,000 people. The preacher was an
up and coming televangelist with a virtual encyclopedic knowl-
edge of Bible prophecy and current events in the Middle East—
not to mention a man with friends in very high places.

My ears perked up immediately when the preacher shifted to
talking about Iraq and Afghanistan. Knowing the bloodshed and
the chaos in Iraq and the admission of the Bush administration

that the war had been mismanaged, I wanted to hear a seasoned Christian minister shed some light on the issue. As the crowd was building momentum with amens and hallelujahs, the preacher started by saying that historically every time God wants His kingdom to advance in areas resistant to the gospel, He sends a war first. The preacher continued to stir the crowd by talking about TVs beaming the gospel in Afghanistan and soldiers distributing tapes and CD's of *his* messages to civilians in Iraq. According to the preacher, these were clear signs of success.

With nods of approval and the occasional applause from the crowd, the preacher continued with the story of an e-mail he had received from an Iranian university student pleading with him to "Tell Bush to bomb us." The preacher's message couldn't have been clearer. God wants the U.S. to go to war against Iran. While the crowd laughed at the preacher's condescending remarks aimed at those opposed to the Iraq war, I couldn't help but wonder if anyone else in the room was concerned with the fact that here was a Christian minister advocating the use of force to spread the gospel. The preacher was calling for Holy War—and no one seemed to notice.

In the months preceding the invasion of Iraq, I, along with millions of other American Christians, reasoned to myself that since democracy brings religious freedom, the invasion of Iraq would be a righteous invasion because it would open the door of freedom for Iraqis to hear the gospel. When I returned home from London, after staring face to face with a man willing to take up the sword with an equal conviction that God was on his side, I couldn't get the gnawing question out of my mind. If Christianity values religious freedom and religious freedom leads to democracy, would Jesus then support a war of aggression in order to advance the cause of democracy?

The question is far from irrelevant. Before the invasion of Iraq, our nations' leaders told us that the Iraqis would greet us as liberators and nearly everyone that I knew believed them. It wasn't long after the fall of Saddam that we started hearing some Iraqis calling for an Islamic state and referring to U.S. personnel as occupiers and crusaders. Most people I knew were shocked and offended, and for understandable reasons. We in America believe that freedom and democracy are God's gifts to the world. Our schools, our churches, our holidays and our public institutions reinforce the idea that political freedom is a value worth fighting for. Whether religious or non-religious, the average American is culturally conditioned to believe in certain inalienable rights that all men are entitled to, and if those rights are denied, it's time to pick up the sword and fight—with God's blessing.

Very few of us think of fighting for freedom and democracy as Holy War, but whether we realize it or not, that's exactly how a significant portion of the Muslim world sees it. Logical fallacies aside, Khalid's arguments could be summarized in three short sentences: Christianity leads to democracy. Democracy is man-made law. Man-made law leads to chaos. Whether we like it or not, this is an argument that millions of Muslims around the world, even the less radical ones find compelling. For them, words like "freedom" and "democracy" mean pornography and partial birth abortion. Democracy is convicted murderers and child molesters serving a few years in prison and then being set free to roam the streets again. Freedom means gambling, miniskirts, and legalized drugs. In short, democracy is man-made law, which is a mockery, something that's totally flexible, open to the whims and interpretations of the society, while their law is supposedly from God. We believe in the virtue of fighting for freedom and democracy while they believe in the virtue of fighting to make God's law the law of the land. We believe God's on our side. So do they.

One of the things Khalid continued to bring up in our conversation was the medieval Crusades. Every time Khalid brought this up, I emphasized that Jesus would not have supported the crusades. And then Khalid would reply with, "What do you think is happening in Iraq and Afghanistan? George Bush has launched a crusade against Islam." To that I would reply, "But no one is preaching Christianity and forcing Muslims to be baptized. And if they did, I would be the first to object. Christians don't believe in the use of the sword to spread the gospel."

It wasn't until I returned home that I started noticing my Christian friends and colleagues saying things like, "Soldiers in Iraq are doing the will of God" or "God told Bush to go to Iraq so that the gospel can be advanced." I even heard a popular Christian talk radio host tell a caller, "Remember, when you serve in the U.S. military, you're serving Jesus." What my friends and colleagues were articulating is a worldview that sees America as a nation set apart by God to advance His Kingdom on the earth. America's cause is God's cause. America is a Christian nation; therefore God fights for America. When America uses the sword, it's always for righteous purposes.

Probably the most articulate Christian leader to express the view of America as God's divine sword bearer is Rod Parsley. In his book *Silent No More,* Parsley lays out a vision for America invoking the spirit of the medieval crusades, and does so without apology. According to Parsley:

"I believe September 11, 2001 was a *generational call to arms that we can no longer ignore.* Consider the evidence. It was to defeat Islam, among other dreams, that Christopher Columbus sailed to the New World in 1492. He was a young boy when the devastating news of the fall of Constantinople to Muslim armies reached his land. It marked him. *He grew into manhood surrounded by tales of the Crusades into Muslims lands.* When he determined to fulfill Marco Polo's dream and return to the east by sailing west, he did so in part to harvest the wealth of the New World to liberate the Old World from Islam... Columbus dreamed of defeating the armies of Islam with the armies of Europe made mighty by the wealth of the New World. It was this dream that, in part, became America. What Columbus dreamed became the hope of later generations" (italics emphasis mine). [5]

Tales of crusades into Muslim lands? Harvesting the wealth of the new world to defeat the armies of Islam? If this kind of militant language disturbs you, it should. Parsley's book has been heavily

---

[5] *Silent No More* (Charisma House, 2005), 90–91

promoted in the evangelical world both here in the United States and around the world. In one short page, Parsley called for a revival of the medieval crusades and, rather than making the headline news, few seem to notice. How is it that Christian leaders can boast about the loving gentle nature of their Savior and then go on to rally their fellow Christians to pick up the sword and fight?

I believe that for too long the word "evangelical" has been synonymous with hyper-nationalism. We've turned the Lord Jesus Christ, the Savior of the world, into a tribal deity who fights for the U.S. flag. We've made God into *our* image and transformed Jesus into the defender of American values. Our pastors invoke the name of Christ to bless *our* troops as they head out for battle. We believe God is on *our* side because America's cause and God's cause are one. Those who oppose our nation's values are *God's* enemies; therefore, we have a right to destroy them.

Author Greg Boyd puts it this way:

"What gives the connection between Christianity and politics such strong emotional force in the U.S.? I believe it is the long-standing myth that America is a Christian nation. From the start, we have tended to believe that God's will was manifested in the conquest and founding of our country—and that it is still manifested in our actions around the globe. Throughout our history, most Americans have assumed our nation's causes and wars were righteous and just, and that 'God is on our side.' In our minds—as so often in our sanctuaries—the cross and the

American flag stand side by side. Our allegiance to God tends to go hand in hand with our allegiance to country... " [6]

The problem with confusing the Kingdom of God, which always looks like Jesus on the cross suffering for the sake of His enemies, with a version of the kingdom of this world, even if it's a new and improved version, is when we enshrine national pride with religious legitimacy, it's bound to produce an unhealthy militarism, especially in a nation that happens to be the world's sole superpower. [7]

Consider the speeches that former president George Bush gave during the aftermath of 9/11 and the subsequent invasions of Afghanistan and Iraq. The man who the media has dubbed "the evangelical president" consistently employed religious language to legitimize the projection of American military power—and often to cheering evangelical crowds. In a speech that Bush gave on the first anniversary of September 11th at Ellis Island, the former president declared:

"The ideal of America is the hope of all mankind... That hope still lights our way. And the light shines in the darkness. And the darkness has not overcome it." [8]

---

6 *Myth of a Christian Nation*, (Zondervan, 2005), 12

7 Tony Campolo, *Speaking My Mind: The Radical Evangelical Prophet Tackles the Tough Issues Christians Are Afraid to Face*, (Nashville: W Publishing Group, a division of Thomas Nelson, Inc. 2004)

8 The full text of this speech can be found at http://news.bbc.co.uk/2/hi/americas/2252515.stm Accessed July 17th, 2008

Biblically literate Christians will recognize the similarity between Bush's quote and John 1:5, which says, "And the light shines in the darkness, and the darkness did not comprehend it." The difference between Bush's use of the phrase and the Apostle John's use of the phrase is Bush was referring to America and the Apostle John was referring to Christ. Identifying America with Christ smacks of political idolatry and, while some evangelical leaders criticized the president at the time, they were few and far between.

Here's another example. In the 2003 State of the Union address, just a few months before the invasion of Iraq, the president told the nation:

"The need is great. Yet there's power, wonder-working power in the goodness and idealism and faith of the American people." [9]

Those of us raised in the Pentecostal/charismatic tradition immediately recognized the signal the president was giving to his evangelical base. The phrase "power, wonder-working power" is reminiscent of a classic hymn penned by Lewis E. Jones which sings, "There is power, power, wonder-working power in the blood of the Lamb." Once again, Bush identified America with Christ. Just as the blood of Christ saves the world, so the blood of American soldiers will save Iraq. The message couldn't have been clearer—and more shocking.

---

9 The full text of Bush's 2003 State of the Union speech can be found at http://www.whitehouse.gov/news/releases/2003/01/20030128-19.html Accessed July 17th, 2008

Contrast President Bush's endorsement of God as the sanctifier of American power with Abraham Lincoln's view of the relationship between God and the military. Even though Lincoln believed freeing the slaves and preserving the union was a just cause, Lincoln never claimed that the Lord was on his side. Instead, Lincoln said, "I know that the Lord is always on the side of the right. But it is my constant anxiety and prayer that I and this nation should be on the Lords side." [10] Instead of *presuming* that he and the nation were in the right, Lincoln *prayed* that he and the nation were in the right. What a tragedy that our nation's spiritual leaders have so drastically abandoned Lincoln's humble approach! Could it be that our nation's spiritual leaders have so mixed their devotion to Christ with devotion to the State that the two are barely distinguishable?

As a missionary who has traveled the world many times over, something that has troubled me for a long time is the discrepancy between the way we as Americans view ourselves and the way much of the rest of the world views us. Nowhere is the contrast more vivid than when it comes to our nation's actions around the globe. When it comes to the projection of American power, we believe our intentions are always good and virtuous while much of the rest of the world believes America looks out primarily for it's self-interest.

We in America tend to believe that our nation's values are universal values. What's good for America is good for the world. What's bad for America is bad for the world. Enemies of America are

---

10 http://www.quotedb.com/authors/abraham-lincoln/quote Accessed 12/20/07

humanity's enemies. God fights for America because America is on the side of freedom and democracy. America is blessed with wealth and prosperity because America is a nation founded on Biblical principles, not because America sometimes uses its military power along with international lending institutions like the IMF and the World Bank to bully impoverished countries into submission. America won the cold war because God is on the side of capitalism, not because our nation spent billions of dollars to install murderous dictators friendly to American interests in places like Latin America, Southern Africa, and Southeast Asia. We honor those who fight under the banner of the U.S. flag, even if the war isn't logically tied to legitimate self-defense, with the same fervor as we honor Christian missionaries who die as martyrs for the cause of Christ. In Holy America, the Kingdom of God and the Kingdom of the Sword go hand in hand.

The irony in all of this is that millions of non-Westerners around the world—especially those in the Muslim world—don't think of us as a Christian nation. They think of us as a godless nation. In their minds, they see us as a nation that talks the talk but doesn't walk the walk. They see us as a nation whose economic policies are enslaving the world's poor even though our leaders promise trade justice and third world debt cancellation. They see us as greedy and meddlesome when we use our resources to keep corrupt dictators in power throughout the Muslim world and tolerate human rights abuses in their countries that we would never tolerate in our country. They see us as hypocritical when we preach non-proliferation for Iran but not for Israel, when we preach free trade to the rest of the world but then pour billions of dollars a year into agricultural subsidies, when we condemn human rights abuses in China but not in oil-producing Saudi Arabia. [11]

While a sizable portion of Americans view 9/11 as an act of a few crazy radicals seeking to impose their religion and way of life on us (and, to an extent, this is true), it's important to understand that the vast majority of Muslims believe that we in America and the Western world have been imposing our way of life on them for centuries. I think it's important for Christians to remember that not too long ago, our faith became linked to imperialism during the colonial expansion of missionary nations like Spain, Britain, Belgium, and France. During the first era of protestant missions, Christianity and colonization went hand in hand. And now democracy is seen by many as the same kind of force, one that comes in the name of peace and love and prosperity, but which will drop bombs on innocent civilians in the name of these virtues.

In America we tend to think of political freedom as a universal value, something that all people everywhere aspire to. I used to think this too until a few years back when I was on a 24-hour train ride in China and a female university student decided to practice her English by engaging me in conversation. After a few minutes of small talk, the young woman started to tell me how much she admired Mao Zedong, the brutal communist dictator that killed

---

11 Meic Pearse, *Why the Rest Hates the West* (Intervarsity Press, 2004), 36

millions of people but is highly regarded in China as the "Great Leader" responsible for China's "Great Leap Forward" into the modern era. Although I tend to shy away from politics in polite conversation, especially when I'm in a foreign country, I couldn't help but ask the woman what she thought about the fact that tens of millions of people died of starvation while Mao was in power. The woman calmly responded, "I think Mao Zedong is the greatest leader in the history of China. He has made our lives better and we have him to thank for it." Clearly, freedom and democracy weren't on the list of this woman's values any more than Khalid's list of values.

Ever since my conversation with the woman on the train, I've thought to myself, "How can a young woman with full possession of her mental capacities develop a value system that says its okay for millions of people to die as long as it serves the good of the State?" In this young woman's mind, the political system she grew up with is not only a cause worth dying for. It's a cause worth *killing* for. I always assumed that it must be because of our Christian heritage in America that we don't think like this young woman, but now that I have the pestering teaching of Jesus rolling around in my head, "Remove the plank from your own eye" I'm asking myself questions I never thought I'd ask. Are we really that much different in our zeal for our political system, democracy and free-market capitalism, as this woman was with her political system, an authoritarian form of socialism? If we frame the question around the issue of the current clash between the West and Islam, then we have to ask ourselves if we in the West have the same type of religious zeal for democracy as Islamists do for political Islam. Is Democracy the new crusade?

If there's one idea that stands firm in the American psyche, it's the idea that America is an exceptional nation that doesn't behave like other nations. America doesn't invade and conquer for wealth and glory like other nations do, and if America does invade a nation, it's always for the good of the people. One of the things that surprised me when I started to examine world history, especially modern history, is that *practically all* imperial powers have believed the same things about themselves. When the British ruled the world under the banner of the queen, they believed that by imposing the British way of life on their subjects, they were doing it for their own good—with God's blessing. The Greeks and the Romans also believed their superior way of life gave them a divine right to invade and conquer. While we may think we're different, the irony is that it's our very belief that we're different that makes us exactly the same as every other imperial nation that has gone before us.

When it comes to war, our nation's political leaders have always set the agenda while Christian leaders have supplied the flags and the crosses. Consider the occupation and annexation of the Philippines that took place at the turn of the last century. During the time President McKinley believed America had a "God-given responsibility to civilize the backward and politically incapable Filipinos." [12] When the Filipinos decided to fight for their independence, American soldiers resorted to torture, indiscriminate killing, devastating crops in uncooperative villages, and even

---

12 *The Wars of America* (Mercer University Press, 1991), 157, 158

herding civilians into camps. In the 1900–1903 War to conquer the Philippines, estimates range anywhere between 250,000 and 1,000,000 civilian casualties. [13] In the midst of that war, U.S. Army General Shefter said: "It may be necessary to kill half of the Filipinos in order that the remaining half of the population may be advanced to a higher plane of life than their present semi-barbarous state affords." [14] It seems like this particular American military general would have a friend in the female university student from China.

In the 20th century, one of the most fervently evangelical presidents in our history, Woodrow Wilson, rallied the American people to enter World War I on the basis that the war would "make the world safe for democracy." Just as many Americans today view the projection of military power into the Muslim world as a contest between the Christian God and the Muslim God, so evangelical leaders at the time viewed the battle as a battle of the gods. In a 1918 issue of the Lutheran Quarterly, one author wrote of the war, "It is a contest in the world of spiritual ideas, a clash between the spirit of the German god Odin and the Christian god as revealed in the character and program of Jesus Christ." Another clergyman called the war a "crusade" that was the "greatest" and "holiest" in

---

13 The lower number comes from *The Wars of America* (Mercer University Press 1991), 159. The higher number comes from an article by Lance Selfa entitled U.S. Imperialism, a Century of Slaughter. http://www.thirdworldtraveler.com/American_Empire/Century_Imperialism.html
Accessed July 18th, 2008

14 ibid

history. [15] Even the great evangelist Billy Sunday said, "The man who breaks all the rules but at last dies fighting in the trenches is better than you God-forsaken mutts who won't enlist." [16]

Besides the fact that World War I was one of the bloodiest wars in world history, it was a direct result of the harsh reparations that Germany had to pay in the aftermath of World War I that led to World War II, and it was the deal that FDR struck with Stalin at the end of World War II that directly led to the Cold War between capitalism and communism that lasted another 45 years. And it's precisely the aftermath of the Cold war that has led to the current crisis between the West and Islam—all this from the war that was supposed to make the world safe for democracy!

Let's talk about the Cold War. In June of 2002, I was in the country of Laos when I noticed a T-shirt with a full-sized portrait of Osama Bin-Laden. Since this was a few short months after 9/11, I was shocked and angry, like every American would be. It wasn't until later that I found out about the U.S. bombing campaign that devastated the country of Laos during the Vietnam War era, killing thousands of civilians. Even more appalling is the fact that people in Laos are still dying today as a result of unexploded bombs and landmines stemming from the same invasion. In the name of democracy the U.S. dropped two to three times as many bombs on Laos, Vietnam, and Cambodia than all the bombs dropped on

---

15 ibid
16 ibid

Western Europe during World War II. [17] In Vietnam alone, the U.S. sprayed 3.5 *million* acres of land with defoliants, with effects lasting up to 100 years. Even today, children are born deformed because of what took place decades ago. And this doesn't include the approximately 1.5 million Vietnamese killed (including 587,000 civilians) and the 1.5 million people wounded during the conflict—all in the name of advancing the cause of democracy. [18]

And this is just one small peninsula in Southeast Asia. The situation gets even more ghastly when you consider other regions of the world. In the name of economic "freedom", the U.S. has poured tens of millions of dollars into supporting tyrants like Mobutu in Zaire, Pinochet in Chile, the Shah in Iran, and Suharto in Indonesia. Each of these men routinely tortured and killed political opponents while receiving a green light from the U.S.— and these are just a *few* of the murderous dictators the U.S. has supported over the years, and still continues to support, in the name of "freedom" (aka….free market capitalism). This doesn't even include countries we've *invaded* in the name of "freedom." In the hundred years since the Spanish civil war, the U.S. has invaded Cuba five times, Honduras four times, Panama four times, the Dominican Republic twice, Haiti twice, Nicaragua twice and Grenada once. [19] More recently we invaded Afghanistan and Iraq in the name of democracy, and this doesn't

---

17 This statistic comes from Errol Morse's 2004 award winning documentary *The Fog of War*

18 http://www.ausvets.powerup.com.au/vietnam/vietstat.htm, Accessed July 18th, 2008

19 http://www.isreview.org/issues/07/century_of_slaughter.shtml,

include the plethora of governments the U.S. has overthrown covertly through CIA sponsored coups.

As much as I enjoy freedom and democracy, I believe an agenda to democratize the world at the barrel of a gun is grounded in false presuppositions. An examination of American history will reveal that, ever since the Pilgrims landed on the Mayflower, America has perceived itself to be an exceptional nation with a divine mandate to spread its values to the rest of the world. Many of the Pilgrims believed that while they were establishing their colonies, they were building a "New Jerusalem", a nation destined to become a "City on a Hill", a beacon of light to the rest of the world. Although the majority of the Founding Fathers replaced the Puritanical views of the early pilgrims with enlightenment values, they nevertheless maintained the missionary ethos of their ancestors. They believed they were establishing a nation that would lead the world into a new era of peace and harmony. Even today it's ironic that although fundamentalist Christians and secular liberals have sharp disagreements about what constitutes "American" values, there are considerable populations in both camps that agree on the idea that "American" values are worth diffusing to the rest of the world—through force if necessary.

As comforting as it may be to perceive ourselves as a nation set apart by God, a City on a Hill, a light that shines in the darkness, if it can be sufficiently proven that the Bible forbids such a mixture of religion and nationalism, the question that we in America are going to have to ask ourselves is are we a strong enough people to abandon our myths and see the truth, or will we continue to perpetuate the myths in favor of cultural cohesion?

CHAPTER 5

The Absent Revolutionary

I love July 4th. I love the barbecue, the swimming, and the fireworks. I love the red, white, and blue, and the Star-Spangled Banner. I love the fact that I was born in America where I can worship God as I please and not in China or Saudi Arabia where people are thrown in prison merely for possessing a Bible or sharing their faith. I realize that if it wasn't for the Revolutionaries, I could still be living in fear of a British soldier seizing my home and my property. I'm grateful for the sacrifice of the brave soldiers that fought to secure the freedom I now enjoy and never in a million years would I want to do or say anything to disrespect them—which is why I'm faced with a crushing dilemma.

Here's my problem. As an American, I'm proud of our revolutionary ancestors, but as a Christian, I can't find a single basis for violent revolution in the New Testament.

Even more perplexing, I imagine if I were a patriot in the 18th century looking to overthrow the British government through violent revolution, I think the New Testament would be the last place I'd look for inspiration. The emperor Nero was one of the worst dictators in human history and yet, what does the Apostle Peter admonish believers living under Nero's insane rule? "Honor all people. Love the brotherhood. Fear God. Honor the king" (I Peter 2:17). Not exactly Boston Tea Party material!

The Apostle Paul's revolutionary credentials don't fare much better. If we ask Paul the question of how a Christian should relate to governing authorities, Paul would tell us to pay our taxes, obey the laws of the land, and to pray for our leaders (Romans 13:1–7, I Timothy 2:1–3). More specifically, if we ask Paul the question of whether a Christian should participate in violent revolution to overthrow an existing power the answer is a resounding no! The Apostle's instructions are clear.

"Therefore whoever resists the authority resists the ordinance of God, and those who resist will bring judgment on themselves" (Romans 13:2).

The word *resist* in this passage is *anthistemi* in the Greek, and it refers specifically to armed resistance. The message would have been unmistakably clear to Paul's original recipients. Don't rebel against Rome! The Apostle didn't want his students engaging in violent revolution, even though the proposed revolution was against an evil empire that crucified the Lord Jesus Christ.

Not only did Paul discourage violent revolution, when we examine the writings of the apostles, including the gospel narratives in their socio-political context, practically *the entire New Testament* can be described as a cautionary tale against violent revolution. When Jesus said, "Agree with your adversary quickly" (Matthew 5:25), He was telling His followers not to antagonize their *Roman* adversaries. When Jesus said, "There is nothing covered that will not be revealed, nor hidden that will not be known," (Luke 12:2) He was talking about conspiracies to oust the Romans. When Jesus told His disciples, "Pray that your flight will not happen in winter," (Mark 13:18) He was talking about the destruction of the temple in 70 A.D. and how in the not-too-distant future, His followers would have to flee Jerusalem as a result of the Jewish leaders not heeding His advice. [20] The contrast between Jesus and the Jewish revolutionaries couldn't be greater. Jesus allowed Himself to be crucified by the Roman authorities and, on the third day, was gloriously resurrected. The Jewish revolutionaries led a revolt against Rome and in the end they lost the city, the temple, and as the tragedy of Mosada shows, their lives.

The Apostle Paul "turned the world upside down" (Acts 17:6) when He traveled the Roman Empire preaching the gospel of Christ's crucifixion and resurrection, but for those preoccupied with changing an existing social order through violent revolution, Paul's advice might be considered to be disappointing. I'm afraid that neither John Brown, Thomas Jefferson nor Che Guvera

---

20 The notes in this paragraph come from a workshop I attended at Cornerstone Festival 2007 with Wheaton Professor Nicholas Parron

would find Paul's advice to Kingdom of God citizens very appealing, especially when it comes to admonitions like, "Aspire to lead a quiet life, to mind your own business, and to work with your own hands" (I Thessalonians 4:11).

Jesus could have shown the world's impoverished masses how to stick it to their oppressors by leading a revolt against the Romans, and, make no mistake about it, overthrowing the Romans would have been a "just cause", but He deliberately chose not to. Instead He chose to associate with the humble by becoming a son of a carpenter and hanging out with tax collectors and fishermen. Even more baffling is the fact that Jesus went out of His way to show His followers that their oppressors were people too. Imagine what a kick in the side His disciples must have felt when Jesus spoke of a *Roman centurion* as having greater faith than anyone He had seen in all of Israel (Matthew 8:10). Jesus refused to stigmatize people based on their status or position in life— even if the particular position was that of a foreign occupier!

Rather than opting for Caesar-style violent revolution, Jesus opted for the gradual approach. When describing the nature of His Kingdom, Jesus made it clear that a Kingdom of God lifestyle may seem to accomplish very little in terms of tangible results in the short run, but Kingdom of God citizens shouldn't be discouraged, even if they remain penniless and powerless because:

"The Kingdom of heaven is like a mustard seed, which a man took and sowed in his field, which indeed is the least of all the seeds; but when it is grown it is greater than the herbs and becomes a

tree, so that the birds of the air come and nest in its branches"
(Matthew 13:31–32).

Although Jesus expected His followers to make a positive contribution to society, He knew there were no shortcuts to solving the
world's problems through Caesar-style power grabs, even if the
reigning power deserved to be overthrown. Revolution Jesus-
style is far more subtle—and effective. Nowhere is this clearer
than in the famous passage in the Sermon on the Mount that says:

"You have heard that it was said, 'An eye for an eye and a tooth for
a tooth.' But I tell you not to resist an evil person. But whoever
slaps you on the right cheek, turn the other to him also. If anyone
wants to sue you and take away your tunic, let him have your
cloak also. And whoever compels you to go one mile, go with him
two" (Matthew 5:38–41).

It's a shame how often this passage is misconstrued to be saying
that Jesus wants His followers to roll over and play dead in the
face of evil. Nothing can be further from the truth! In this passage,
Jesus used a similar word for "resist" that the Apostle Paul used
in Romans 13:2 when speaking of not resisting the Roman authorities. According to New Testament scholar Walter Wink, the word
for "resist" in this passage is *antistenai* and it means more than
simply to "stand against" or "resist." It means to resist violently. [21]
Jesus wasn't saying to His followers don't resist evil at all. He
was saying don't resist evil *with violence.* Don't respond in like

---

21 Walter Wink, *Jesus and Nonviolence: A Third Way* (Fortress Press 2003), 11

manner to the offense. According to Jesus, Kingdom of God citizens are called to resist evil, but the qualification is nonviolently.

Far from teaching His followers to be doormats, Jesus was actually giving oppressed people everywhere a way to stand up for themselves. By asserting their humanity over and against the inhumanity of their oppressors, Jesus taught His followers how to turn the tables on their oppressors by defying the status quo. Notice that Jesus said, "If someone slaps you on the *right* cheek, turn the other to him also." Why not the left cheek? The answer is because in a right-handed society, if you want to slap someone on their right cheek, you have to use the back of your hand, and in the culture at the time, a back handed slap was an insulting way of putting a person of lower standing in their place. By turning the other cheek, the victim forces the slapper to confront him as an equal, denying their superior the right to humiliate them. [22]

The same is true of Jesus' admonition to unfortunate peasants to strip naked if someone wanted to sue them for their tunic. In Jewish law, if a creditor put a debtor in a position of having to choose between his clothes and his debt, the shame would go to the creditor, not to the naked man (Exodus 22:26–27, Deuteronomy 24:12–13). Likewise, going the extra mile with a Roman soldier was a hilarious way of putting a power-hungry soldier eager to humiliate his subjects in an awkward position. Rome didn't want their soldiers antagonizing the civilian population too much. That's why they limited the distance a soldier could force a

---

[22] ibid

civilian to carry their load to only one mile. Jesus was essentially teaching his followers how to lampoon their oppressors so they could see the errors of their ways and repent.

Walter Wink in his groundbreaking book *Jesus and Nonviolence* put it this way:

"Jesus in effect is sponsoring clowning. In so doing he carries on a venerable tradition in Judaism. As a later saying of the Talmud runs, 'If a neighbor calls you an ass, put a saddle on your back.' The Powers That Be literally stand on their dignity. Nothing depotentiates them faster than deft lampooning. By refusing to be awed by their power, the powerless are emboldened to seize the initiative, even where structural change is not possible. This message, far from being a counsel for perfection unattainable in this life, is a practical, strategic measure for empowering the oppressed. It provides a hint of how to take on the entire system in a way that unmasks its essential cruelty and to burlesque its pretensions to justice, law, and order. Here is a poor man who will no longer be treated as a sponge to be squeezed by the rich. He accepts the laws as they stand, pushes them to the point of absurdity, and reveals them for what they really are. He strips nude, walks out before his compatriots, and leaves the creditor and the whole economic edifice he represents, stark naked."

As fun as it may be to dream of creative non-violent strategies to bring oppressors to their knees, perhaps the most common objection to the idea of creative nonviolence as an alternative to Caesar-style revolution is what happens if it doesn't work? What happens if non-violent resistance fails to achieve its objectives? As the cases of

Tiananmen Square in China and the brutal crackdown of Burmese monks in Myanmar show, non-violent resistance doesn't always achieve tangible objectives. Sometimes non-violent initiatives for social justice can actually worsen the situation by provoking fierce resistance from repressive regimes. Sometimes the results achieved from downtrodden masses turning the other cheek can be minimal at best, especially if nothing changes over a lifetime. Doesn't it somehow negate the teachings of Jesus when small acts of defiance over a prolonged period of time fail to achieve lasting results?

If nonviolence were simply a ploy to manipulate the Powers That Be to bend to the will of oppressed masses, the answer would be yes. But for Jesus, non-violence isn't simply a means to achieve an end; non-violence *is* the end. Turning the other cheek and going the extra mile are inseparable from the challenge of loving your enemies. By modeling a lifestyle of radical non-violence, Jesus showed that a willingness to sacrifice for the sake of one's enemies, even if it means suffering grave injustices, is the highest order of the divine life attainable by human beings, *regardless* of the results. At the cross, Jesus suffered the greatest injustice in human history and, rather than threatening retaliation, He cried, "Father forgive them, for they know not what they do." Jesus wasn't motivated by results. He was motivated by love. By allowing Himself to be crucified at the hands of the Roman Empire, Jesus forever freed Kingdom of God citizens from the need to measure the value of suffering redemptive love against tangible worldly ends. The Kingdom of God isn't about achieving. It's about being.

That being said, if we absolutely *have* to measure Jesus-style non-violent resistance against Caesar-style revolution through the sword, history shows that non-violent resistance often proves to be quite effective. The immediate examples that come to mind are Ghandi's revolution in India, a revolution that liberated hundreds of millions of people from the British and Martin Luther King's civil rights movement that ended the humiliating Jim Crow segregation laws in the South. In 1989, 13 nations, totaling a staggering 1.6 billion people, were liberated from communist rule as a result of non-violent resistance, the most notable being Lech Walesa's Solidarity movement in Poland which precipitated the fall of the Soviet Empire. In the 20th century, 3.3 billion people were liberated from oppressive regimes through non-violent revolutions. So much for the charge that non-violence doesn't work! [23]

Another problem with the argument that non-violent resistance is ineffective because of the harsh reaction it can provoke is why should we apply the objection only to non-violence? Why not apply the same results criteria to violent resistance? If it's true that *sometimes* non-violent resistance provokes a harsh reaction from ruling powers, it's equally true that *most of the time*, violent resistance produces an even harsher reaction. Just ask people living in Darfur or Kosovo. In both places, armed resistance has led to barbaric retaliation. And who can forget the Shias and the Kurds that revolted against Saddam Hussein after Gulf One at the behest of Bush Sr? Again. Tens of thousands killed. The list goes on and on.

---

23 Walter Wink, as quoted by Susan Ives in a 2001 talk.
http://en.wikipedia.org/wiki/Nonviolence Accessed July 18th, 2008

History shows that more often than not, armed revolt doesn't work out too well for would be revolutionaries, and even if revolutionaries get what they want, usually the regime that comes to power ends up mirroring the evil they replace. The French revolted against the monarchy and ended up with Napoleon. The Bolsheviks revolted against the Czar and ended up with Lenin and Stalin. Why should that surprise us? The problem with violent revolution is the simple fact that revolutionaries must rely on brute force to seize power and then turn around and declare illegal the same violence that brought them to power. Violence begets violence. It's the name of the game.

Let me make it perfectly clear that nothing I've written so far means that Christians can't recognize the occasional good that's been accomplished through war or revolution, whether it be our own wars or that of others. A commitment to nonviolence doesn't mean that we can't recognize that black people are better off after the Civil War than they were before; nor does it mean that we have to rewrite history to paint our nation and those who have fought for our nation in the worst possible light. Kingdom of God citizens know that even though the world's system of power through the sword is under the dominion of Satan, that God always has the upper hand and remains sovereign over the nations, using all things to accomplish as much good as possible in a fallen world.

As I stated at the beginning of the chapter, I love the 4th of July and I can honestly say that I wouldn't want to be born and raised in any other nation, but now that I've seen Jesus and the Apostles, and for that matter the entire New Testament, in a new light, I can't help but rethink our nation's history and wonder if things could have been different.

Is it inevitable that had there been no revolution, our nation would have remained under the thumb of the British? It's possible, but we don't really know that. Canada and Australia are highly successful first world democracies and neither of them achieved their national sovereignty through violent revolution. Yes, they remain a part of the British Commonwealth, but how likely is it that war is going to break out any time soon between Canada or Australia and the UK? The answer should be obvious. Canada and Australia received their freedom gradually.

Is it possible the U.S.A. could have been in the same position as Canada or Australia is today had our forefathers opted for a gradual approach? We'll never know. The British Empire is now a chapter for the history books, but the irony is, with over 700 bases in 130 plus countries around the world, the new empire on the world stage is the U.S.A. [24] The economic, military, and political clout of the U.S. empire dwarfs that of the British Empire and, right or wrong, there are many around the world who feel they need to be freed from the clutches of American dominance. All of this has happened despite the fact that the last thing the Founding Fathers wanted was to create an empire to police the world. As we've already seen, this shouldn't surprise us. Violent revolutions tend to produce the same types of governments they overthrow, even if it takes a while. It's how the world's power-over system works.

---

24 *Christianity and War* (Vance Publications, 2005)

I'm glad that slaves are freed and the union is preserved, but I wonder if the staggering 620,000 lives that were lost during the Civil War was necessary. [25] The Bible says, "The wrath of man does not produce the righteousness of God" (James 1:20). What if the North and the South could have gotten together and discussed how to make it economically feasible for southern landowners to free their slaves? What if there had been more white people willing to risk their lives to help slaves escape their masters by working the Underground Railroad? More importantly, what if the majority of Christians at the time would have demonstrated the same commitment to racial integration in their churches as the early Christians did in the Book of Acts? In mainstream evangelicals circles nowadays, the idea that white people and black people are supposed to worship, pray, and celebrate the Lord's Supper together is old news, but that's *now*. What if that would have been the consensus *then?* Would slavery have been an issue if the majority of Caucasian Christians at the time had viewed their fellow countrymen of African descent as equal brothers in Christ? Again, we'll never know.

One thing we do know is the brutality of the Civil War and the economic hardships of the Reconstruction era that followed left a sour taste in a lot of people's mouths, and that's exactly what gave rise to the KKK and Jim Crow segregation laws. The war may have freed the slaves, but it did little to free the former slave-masters from their hatred and their prejudice. It's hard for late Gen Xers like myself to imagine that it wasn't too long ago

---

25 http://www.civilwarhome.com/casualties.htm Accessed July 18th, 2008

that groups like the KKK ruled entire regions of the country, able to get away with the most horrific crimes because the local mayor and the police secretly backed them. In many cases, the KKK would even walk into churches during a Sunday morning service, white robe and all, and recruit the deacons and the elders, with the pastor's tacit approval. Nowadays, few people view the term skinhead in a positive light, even in the Deep South.

Shortly after Hurricane Katrina struck southern Mississippi, I saw on the evening news a story about a white supremacist group offering bags of food to their fellow white countrymen and, to their great surprise, they couldn't find any takers. Nobody wanted to accept food from a group handing out groceries to white people only. If this incident had happened 40 or 50 years ago, I think the reaction would have been much different. Yes, there's still white on black racism in the Deep South, but not on the same level as the racism depicted in *To Kill a Mockingbird* or *Mississippi Burning*. Few people nowadays want to be identified as racist, even if that's what they really are deep down. Contrast this with 50 years ago when the term "nigger-lover" was the insult people avoided the most.

Even the most ardent pessimist has to admit that today's racial atmosphere is better than it was in the 1960's. The question is how was this accomplished? I believe it was the non-violent witness of Martin Luther King and the civil rights movement. As white people everywhere watched black people on their TV screens marching courageously toward the attack dogs and the fire hoses, refusing to defend themselves against their oppressors, something changed in the heart of the nation, and the nation hasn't been the same since. Unlike the Civil War, which merely created a legal document to free the slaves, King's non-violent revolution didn't just free the slaves, it freed the slave masters as well, and all of us are better off because of it.

This brings us back to the Apostle Paul. As I mentioned earlier in the chapter, when it comes to fomenting violent revolution to bring about social change, Paul's revolutionary credentials would be very disappointing to someone like John Brown, a white man who led a revolt against slavery that proved instrumental in sparking the Civil War. His advice would have little appeal for Thomas Jefferson, a self-professed deist and a skeptic of divine revelation. Latin American socialist revolutionaries like Che Guvera would have a hard time with Paul as well.

If we're looking for ways to legitimize violent revolution in Paul's writings, we'll end up sorely disappointed. But if we're looking for revolution, we needn't look any further than, "There is neither Jew nor Greek, there is neither slave nor free, there is neither male nor female; for you are all one in Christ Jesus" (Galatians 3:28). The revolutionary nature of God's Kingdom is that Kingdom of God citizens refuse to define human existence in the same way the world does. The world defines human existence primarily in terms of struggle, be it racial struggle, class struggle, or gender struggle, black versus white, Jews versus Palestinians, Palestinians versus Jews, natives versus Foreign Occupiers, the proletariat versus the bourgeoisee, women versus men. Struggles between the oppressors and the oppressed have led to untold bloodshed throughout the millennia and have defined human existence ever since Adam and Eve ate the forbidden fruit. It's a vicious cycle where the lines between victim and criminal, innocent and guilty are often blurred at the barrel of a gun.

The brilliance of the Kingdom of God is that Kingdom of God citizens refuse to view themselves and their fellow man based on earthly distinctions. In New Testament times, this meant that a slave no longer had to view himself as inferior just because he was a slave and neither did a master have the right to view himself as superior just because he was a master. It meant that Jews didn't need to feel themselves inferior to the Roman soldiers that occupied their land and neither should the soldiers see themselves as superior. Rather than striving to change the power over institutions created by earthly kingdoms, the Kingdom of God creates a new community on the earth that ignores the very race, class, and gender distinctions that power the institutions. The role of the Church is to call men and women out from the world's power-over system and into a community in which Gentiles are equal with Jews, slaves are equal with kings, and women are equal with men. To the extent that the community of the Church practices radical equality through forgiveness, self-sacrifice, and bearing each other's burdens, the Church serves as a witness to the outside world, exposing the insufficiencies of institutionalized power as a way of managing human behavior.

The problem with trying to overthrow the powers that be, is the very act of trying to overthrow them gives them way too much credit. Caesar-style power grabs actually *validate* the powers that be because they assume their worldview, namely that power over others is something to be desired and that powerful is superior to powerless. The beauty of Jesus' upside down kingdom is that citizens of the Kingdom flat out ignore earthly distinctions based on stupid notions such as powerful equals superior and powerless equals inferior. If only more human beings would ignore such distinctions how peaceful the world would be!

In Habu Abu Assad's frighteningly realistic 2005 film "Paradise Now," two young Palestinian men consider blowing themselves up as suicide bombers because they would rather kill than continue living under the thumb of—ironically—*Israeli* soldiers that treat them as inferiors. How tragic it is that men such as these are unaware that a Kingdom exists in which the poor and the powerless are the exalted ones and the rich and the powerful are the humiliated ones! (James 1:9–10) This is why the New Testament forbids violent revolution. Violent revolution simply isn't revolutionary enough.

CHAPTER 6

Iron Jesus and Sweet Sister Sally

S weet Sister Sally is the most gentle and compassionate person you'll ever meet. Every week, Sweet Sister Sally goes to church, pays her tithes, volunteers at the local food pantry, and spends hours on her knees praying for America, the nations, and lost souls around her. If you're ever in a bind, Sweet Sister Sally is always there to lend a helping hand. Sweet Sister Sally radiates the love of Jesus to everyone around her. If you ask her about the greatest love in her life, Sweet Sister Sally will gladly tell you about her Lord and Savior Jesus Christ and how He wants everyone to experience the Heavenly Father's love through Him—no matter who they are or what they've done.

If we evaluate Sweet Sister Sally on the basis of her kindness and personal devotion, then who could dispute that Sweet Sister Sally is a saint? Jesus said, "Be wise as serpent and harmless as doves," (Matthew 10:16). Not only is Sweet Sister Sally wise as a serpent in her counsel to the poor and the downtrodden, but on nearly every account, Sweet Sister Sally seems to fit the description of what it means to be harmless as a dove—that is until you probe a litter deeper into her beliefs and ask yourself what the state of the world would be like if *everyone* believed the way Sweet Sister Sally believes. This is where things begin to get a little murky.

Sweet Sister Sally believes the War on Terror is an epic battle between the God of the Bible and the god of the Koran. In this epic battle between the warring gods, America and Israel are always on the side of good and anyone who questions the projection of either country's military power is squarely in the devil's camp. According to Sweet Sister Sally, all Muslims are potential terrorists, peacemaking between Jews and Palestinians is the work of the anti-Christ, and the U.S. invasion of Iraq was exclusively to protect Americans from Osama and innocent Iraqis from Saddam—and if anyone disagrees with her analysis it's probably because either they don't know God or they've been duped by Oprah. If Sweet Sister Sally hears of a candidate or activist advocating for peace in the Middle East or arguing for a U.S. foreign policy that works within the framework of international law, Sweet Sister Sally goes fast to her knees.

As an American Christian reared in the Pentecostal/charismatic movement, I've spent a lifetime admiring the Sweet Sister Sallies of this world. These are the ones who have loved me, prayed for me, and encouraged me to do great things for God since the time I was a small child. My charismatic heritage has exposed me to some of the most gracious and gentle people I could ever meet. These are men and women who love God, embrace sinners, and live their lives the best that they know how—and that's exactly why I'm so conflicted as I write. The last thing I want to be is a divisive Christian with a chip on my shoulder, taking cheap shots at everyone who disagrees with me and forgetting all the wonderful qualities about the people who have shaped my life—as if I have no more to learn from them. At the same time, I want my friends, family, and spiritual mentors to understand where I'm coming from and why I think things need to change—even if they continue to disagree with me. So if anything I write seems a bit on the critical side, know that at least it's my intention to speak the truth in love.

So here goes...

The strange thing I've noticed about Sweet Sister Sally, Faithful Fred, Joyful Joe, and Compassionate Carl—the beautiful people I've grown up with in the charismatic movement—is when I ask them what's the difference between Jesus and Muhammad, they tell me that Jesus was a man of peace and Muhammad was a man of war. They boast about how Jesus loved His enemies, how He refused to repay evil for evil, and how He sacrificed His life on the cross for the very people that crucified Him, but the moment I even slightly suggest that following Jesus might include having a different attitude about war than Rush Limbaugh or Dick Cheney, then that's when they look at me like I've just flown over the cuckoo's nest. All of the sudden Sweet Sister's Sally's gentle Jesus doesn't seem so gentle anymore. Sweet Sister Sally's Jesus may be harmless as a dove when it comes to loving sinners, but clearly He's a hawk when it comes to war. I often wonder how is it that

Sweet Sister Sally can boast about serving a Savior who loves His enemies on the one hand and then turn around and sanction a holy war on the other hand?

If we're looking for some rhyme or reason to Sweet Sister Sally's strange disconnect, we needn't look any further than the media Sweet Sister Sally consumes on a daily basis. This is where things get *really* strange. Every day Sweet Sister Sally protects herself from the power brokers of secular media by listening to Christian radio, watching Christian television, and reading Christian books by her favorite Christian preachers. The funny thing is rather than urging Sweet Sister Sally to obey the teachings of Jesus to be a peacemaker; these preachers say, "Bomb your enemies," where Jesus says, "Bless your enemies." Where Jesus says, "Turn the other cheek" these preachers say "strike first so you won't have to turn the other cheek." No wonder Sweet Sister Sally is so confused!

At the time of this writing, I'm a 25-year veteran of the charismatic movement, (my dad left the Catholic Church when I was 5). Between going to church, three years of Bible school, 10 years of traveling overseas and countless conferences for Christian leaders, I've probably heard *hundreds* of sermons about the cross. I've heard nearly every type of sermon about how to lay my burdens at the cross, how Jesus purchased my healing at the cross, how I know God loves me because of the cross and, perhaps most importantly, how I need to take up my cross and follow Jesus.

All of these sermons have been wonderful, but what troubles me is, despite the charismatic movement's claim to be the frontrunner in drawing humanity into a deeper relationship with Jesus, I've *never* heard a sermon preached from the pulpit connecting the cross to an ethic of non-violence. I've heard *hundreds* of sermons about what it means to follow Jesus, what it means to imitate Jesus, but *never* a sermon connecting imitating and following Jesus with living a radically non-violent lifestyle—like Jesus. How is it that taking up the cross and following Jesus has come to mean everything *except* for non-violent redemptive love, which is what *actually happened* at the cross?

I believe the vast disconnect between the radical non-violent Jesus of the gospels and the trigger happy Jesus reflected in today's Pentecostal/charismatic circles (and mainstream evangelical theology at large) betrays a false assumption that many people make when approaching Scripture. And that assumption is that Christians should ascribe every passage in the Bible with equal weight and value. If God seems to command a certain type of behavior in the Old Testament and another type of behavior in the New Testament, then we must conclude that the two prescriptions are simply two sides of the same coin. There's just one problem with this assumption. Jesus didn't share it!

Jesus condemned the Scribes and Pharisees for their scrupulous observance of the tithing laws while neglecting the *weightier* matters of the law—justice, mercy, and faith (Matthew 23:23). According to Jesus, some passages are simply weightier than others. Think about what Jesus said when His disciples wanted to call fire down from heaven to consume a disbelieving

Samaritan village. The disciples were obviously referring to the passage in 2 Kings 1:10–12 where Elijah called fire down from heaven to consume King Ahaziah's men. Rather than praising His disciples for aspiring to Elijah-like faith, Jesus rebuked them by saying, "You do not know what manner of spirit you are of." (Luke 9:55–56). Jesus was very comfortable with discarding old ways, even if those ways seemed right at one time. Jesus taught that old wineskins should be *discarded*, not simply patched up (Luke 5:36–39).

In the Old Testament era, God is often portrayed as commanding men to slaughter entire tribes, including women, children, and animals (Deuteronomy 7:1–2,16, I Samuel 15:1–3) and yet throughout His earthly ministry, Jesus never used His power to hurt, to maim, or to kill anyone—including His enemies. When Peter cut off the ear of a man that came to arrest Him, Jesus rebuked Peter and healed the man who wanted to crucify Him! (Luke 22:50–51, John 18:10) Think about what Jesus said to Judas when Judas kissed him with the kiss of betrayal. Rather than striking Him dead, Jesus said, "Friend, why have you come?" (Matthew 26:50). If we cross-reference this with Luke 22:3, we'll discover that Judas was indwelt by *Satan* at this point, and yet Jesus still received His kiss on the cheek and referred to him as *friend!* If we take God's revelation in Jesus seriously, then we have to conclude that God is gracious and kind to even the most demonically inspired human beings.

Jesus referred to the Law of Moses when He said, "You have heard that it was said, 'An eye for an eye and a tooth for a tooth.' But *I* tell you not to resist an evil person." (italics emphasis mine)

(Matthew 5:38) Jesus clearly claimed superiority over Moses. The writer of Hebrews says that Moses was faithful as a servant over his house, but Jesus is the *maker* of the house, that's why Jesus is counted worthy of *much more* glory than Moses (Hebrews 3:2–6). Moses isn't the ultimate standard of grace and truth (John 1:17). Jesus is. Jesus is God. Moses is not.

The same goes for the prophets. The New Testament says, "God, who at various times and in various ways spoke in time *past* to the fathers by the prophets, has in *these last* days spoken to us by His Son," (italics emphasis mine) (Hebrews 1:1–2). When it comes to God's self-revelation to human beings, clearly there's a *then* and there's a *now*. Jesus is the "brightness of His glory and the express image of His person" (Vs 3). The New Testament unequivocally teaches that Jesus is "the image of the invisible God" (Colossians 1:15) and "in Him dwells *all* the fullness of the godhead bodily" (Colossians 2:9). As the Word made flesh (John 1:1,14), Jesus reflects the image and character of God *perfectly* in a way that no one else could ever do—including those who went before Him.

Neither Moses nor the prophets had actually seen God in their lifetimes, but Jesus, as the eternal Son has known the Father's innermost thoughts from all eternity, that's why only He is qualified to express the Father's heart perfectly (John 1:18). Jesus made it clear, "He who has seen me has seen the Father" (John 14:9). If we want to know what God is like—and therefore what God wants us to be like—Jesus is where we start *and* where we finish (Hebrews 12:2).

A common mistake that many people make when reading the stories of Israel's wars in the Old Testament is to try to superimpose them into modern times and use Israel's wars as a justification for modern wars (most often American wars), but this misses the point entirely. Israel's wars weren't *just* wars, they were *holy* wars. The wars that Israel fought were to maintain (and sometimes defend) a racially pure and culturally distinct theocracy. Israel under the Old Covenant was supposed to be directly governed by God. No nation can make that claim today—including modern day Israel. God's theocratic agenda ended at the cross (Ephesians 2:11–18).

While it may be fashionable for Christian leaders to read the Old Testament and use it to justify nearly every projection of military might they can think of, a first century Jew would have thought something entirely different. When a first century Jew read stories about Joshua's army marching around Jericho seven times and walls crashing down (Joshua 6), God sending giant hailstones to defeat the Amorites (Joshua 10:11), or an angel slaying 185,000 Assyrians (2 Kings 19:35), they would have thought to themselves "We don't have to do *anything* but to trust God and let him fight our battles for us." The message of the Old Testament is don't put your trust in military might. That's why God commanded Gideon to fight a super-sized army with only 300 men (Judges 7), and why God was so ticked off with David for numbering his troops (2 Samuel 24:1–9), and why God condemned Asa for making a military alliance with Damascus (2 Chronicles 16:1–10). The theme of Old Testament military history is the battle belongs to God, not man (2 Chronicles 20:15).

Even if we grant that God *sometimes* commanded violence in the Old Testament, it doesn't necessarily follow that God approves of followers of Jesus engaging in acts of violence today. The Prophet Isaiah spoke of a day when God would reveal Himself in a new and different way. In Isaiah 43:19 we read, "Behold, I will do a new thing, now it shall spring forth, shall you not know it?" Jesus fulfilled this prophecy when He said to His disciples, "A *new* commandment I give to you, that you love one another; *as I have loved you*," (John 13:34). The newness of the commandment that Jesus gave His followers isn't simply to love, but to love as I have loved you. The Law commanded human beings to love (Leviticus 19:18), but the problem was nobody knew *the extent* of what love could look like until God showed up in Jesus. Now that Jesus has showed up on the scene, love's standard has been irrevocably lifted. Love always looks like the cross.

Another common objection I get when I attempt to persuade fellow Christians that following Jesus entails a commitment to non-violence is "What about when Jesus said that He didn't come to destroy the law, but to fulfill it?" (Matthew 5:17) My response is usually, "Well—what about it?" There are *gazillions* of interpretations of this verse in scholastic circles, so I'll gladly defer to people smarter than me for that, but whatever this verse means, Jesus *can't* be saying "Disregard what I'm saying for what others said in the past." Jesus subordinated Himself to no one! Jesus said, "If you love me, keep *my* commandments" (italics emphasis mine) (John 14:15).

Jesus recognized that some things in the law reflected God's accommodation to human sinfulness. For example, Jesus despised divorce and yet He recognized that Moses permitted divorce because of the hardness of people's hearts (Matthew 19:8). Jesus despised the institution of slavery (Luke 4:18), and yet, the Law of Moses regulated slavery (Exodus 21, Leviticus 25:44–53, Deuteronomy 23:15–16). God has this funny habit of choosing not to burden people with commandments for which they're not ready (I John 5:3). That's why He waited till the "fullness of time had come" before He sent Jesus (Galatians 4:4). Now that Jesus has come and established the New Covenant, He has made the first covenant—and I quote—"obsolete" (Hebrews 8:13).

Since we're on the subject of Jesus fulfilling the Law, let me suggest another way of looking at how Jesus relates to the Old Testament. Jesus said, "You search the Scriptures, for in them you think you have eternal life; and these are they which testify of Me," (John 5:39). When Jesus read the Old Testament He saw *everything* He read as pointing to Him (Luke 24:27). The Old Testament is the shadow, but Jesus is the substance *behind* the shadow (Colossians 2:16–17, Hebrews 10:1). A shadow is only useful to the degree that it points to the fuller reality of the substance. A shadow itself is incomplete. So if we read the Old Testament and try to impose modern questions of warfare on the text without consulting the reality behind the shadow (Jesus), then we've misread the Old Testament. Even though Moses and the prophets aspired to live perfectly, every single one of them failed at one time or another. One of the ways that Jesus fulfilled the Old Testament was by embodying all the values to which the prophets could only long for, but never deliver.

And one of the dreams the prophets longed for was a world without war. When Jesus proclaimed, "The Kingdom of Heaven is at hand" His Jewish audience would have immediately thought of verses in Isaiah which speak of a day when, "They shall beat their swords into plowshares, and their spears into pruning hooks" when "Nation shall not lift up sword against nation, Neither shall they learn war anymore," (Isaiah 2:4). They probably also thought of the verses which speak of a time when "The wolf also shall dwell with the lamb" (Isaiah 11:6), "The nursing child shall play by the cobra's hole" (Vs 8), and when "They shall not hurt nor destroy in all My holy mountain" (Vs 9). The people were longing for a new age in which creation would be freed from violence and restored to the golden age of Eden. This is why they were so excited when they heard the "good news" of the gospel. They thought a non-violent paradise was going to happen right then and there—through violent revolution.

The problem came when Jesus started saying things like, "Love your enemies, do good to those who hate you, bless those who curse you, and pray for those who spitefully use you" (Luke 6:27). The people were perfectly happy with the prospect of living in a non-violent paradise—once the Romans were ousted from the land—but what they didn't want to do was *become* the change they were looking for. And when Jesus started saying things like, "take up your cross and follow me" (Luke 9:23) and "whoever desires to save his life will lose it, but whoever loses his life for

My sake will save it," (Vs 24), that's when they *really* thought Jesus was out of His mind! Jesus was telling them that if they wanted to live in His non-violent Kingdom, they'd have to be willing to get crucified!

It may have taken them a while, but the Apostles eventually understood what so many in the Church fail to understand today. The cross isn't just a doctrine to be recited on Sunday morning; it's a lifestyle to be lived—a nonviolent lifestyle. Too often we focus on what the cross does for us and we forget that God specifically commands us in His Word to follow the *example* of the cross! Nowhere is this clearer than in I Peter 2:18–23 where Peter instructs servants how to live under cruel taskmasters. In those verses we read:

"Servants, be submissive to your masters with all fear, not only to the good and gentle, but also to the harsh. For this is commendable, if because of conscience toward God one endures grief, suffering wrongfully. For what credit is it if, when you are beaten for your faults, you take it patiently? But when you do good and suffer, if you take it patiently, this is commendable before God. For to this you were called, *because Christ also suffered for us, leaving us an example, that you should follow His steps:* 'Who committed no sin, nor was deceit found in His mouth'; who, when He was reviled, did not revile in return; when He suffered, He did not threaten, but committed Himself to Him who judges righteously;" (italics emphasis mine).

What Peter is saying in this passage is astounding. Peter is saying it's better to suffer *unjustly* than to retaliate. Peter's basis for this is the cross. At the cross, Jesus was reviled but didn't revile in return, Jesus suffered but didn't threaten retaliation. Rather than defend Himself, He submitted even to the point of death and committed Himself to Him who judges righteously. In other words, Jesus left the justice part up to God—like we're supposed to do (Romans 12:19).

Some say that Christians are only supposed to refuse "personal" vengeance, but are free to participate in vengeance against enemies of one's country. But I think limiting the example of Jesus to refusing personal vendettas misses the point entirely. The New Testament repeatedly tells us that we're supposed to imitate Jesus (I Corinthians 11:1, Ephesians 5:1–2, Philippians 2:5–8), that we're supposed to walk just as He walked" (I John 2:6). And if the cross is our example for how we're supposed to live, as the Apostle Peter clearly says it is, then it should be noted that Jesus didn't merely refuse to retaliate against the injustice committed by a single individual; He refused to retaliate against the injustice of the entire Roman Empire!

We see this more clearly in the Garden of Gethsemane. When Jesus was in Gethsemane, He prayed "Father, if it is possible, let this cup pass from me" (Matthew 26:39). We know that the cup that Jesus struggled with was the cup of suffering, but the question should be asked, if the Father had granted Jesus' wish to let the cup pass from him, what would that have looked like? We find the answer in the words that Jesus spoke to Peter after Peter tried to rescue Jesus with the sword, "Put your sword into the sheath. Shall I not drink the cup which My Father has given me?" (John 18:11) The alternative to the Father's cup was violent self-defense.

Jesus could have taken matters into His own hands by calling down "12 legions of angels" to take care of the Romans once and for all (Matthew 27:53). Had He done that, He could have seized the reigns of power and crowned Himself King—just like the people wanted Him to do.

Jesus struggled between two very different options in the garden. Option number one was suffering redemptive love. Option number two was what the world would deem as justified violence. And make no mistake about it, if there is anything that could have qualified as justified violence, then calling down legions of angels to vanquish the bloodthirsty Romans would have qualified. I think that it's easy to forget just how brutal a regime the Roman Empire was. In Luke 13:1 we read that Pilate had actually put some Galileans to death and mingled their blood with their sacrifices— the very sacrifices that God had prescribed in the Law of Moses. (Imagine Hillary Clinton mingling the blood of Republicans with her Diet Coke. I suppose that most of my conservative friends would say that violence would be justified in that instance.) Had Jesus seized the reigns of power and thrown off the yoke of the illegal occupiers, it would have met the criteria for a just cause by any reasonable standard. By choosing the cross, Jesus refused to do what most of us think would have been the courageous thing to do. The world admires freedom fighters. Few admire enemy lovers.

What Jesus did at the cross goes against everything that comes natural to the human mind. I think the real reason why so few Christians think of the cross as providing a non-violent social ethic is because, deep down inside, we think that people who refuse to fight are weak. Real men fight. Only wimps and pansies lay down their arms. I know I'm treading on some sacred cows here, but I think we need to reconsider the idea that "weakness" equals "cowardice" in light of the cross. The Apostle Paul says of Jesus, "For though He was crucified in weakness, yet He lives by the power of God. For we also are weak in Him," (2 Corinthians 13:4). At the cross, Jesus *embraced* weakness. At the cross Jesus *embraced* shame (Hebrews 12:2). Shame and weakness are the two things that men fight the most to avoid being associated with—and these are the very things that Jesus embraced. Jesus won the victory at the cross by bucking the world's value system and turning it on its head. Jesus defeated His enemies by not becoming like them.

Some say that Romans 13:4 provides a basis for Christians participating in state-sanctioned wars since the Apostle Paul says that the government official, "does not bear the sword in vain" and that he is "God's minister, an avenger to execute wrath on him who practices evil." The problem with this argument is just a few verses prior to this passage the Apostle Paul says that Christians are not to avenge themselves, but are to leave vengeance to God (Romans 12:19). Even if we grant that Paul is only prohibiting personal vengeance in this passage (Which I don't accept because Jesus never made a distinction between personal enemies and national enemies), this still doesn't matter because the sword in Romans 13:4 isn't a reference to war. As John Howard Yoder points out in his book *Politics of Jesus:*

"The sword (machaira) is the symbol of judicial authority. It was not the instrument of capital punishment, since the Romans crucified their criminals. It was not the instrument of war since it was but a long dagger. Like the pistol worn by a traffic policeman or the sword worn by a Swiss citizen-officer, it was more a symbol of authority than a weapon."

The point Paul is making in this passage is that God has a sovereign purpose for allowing human governments to exist, therefore Christians are not to participate in violent revolutions. I find it ironic that this is the one passage that just war theorists lean on the most to allow Christians to participate in violence when the actual intent of the passage is to *discourage* Christians from participating in violent revolution. The only argument that can be made in favor of Christians participating in *state-sanctioned* violence from this passage is an argument from silence. The same argument from silence is used to say that since John the Baptist didn't tell Roman soldiers they had to resign, and neither did Peter tell Cornelius he had to quit his job as a Centurion, then that must mean a Christian can be a soldier (Luke 3:14, Acts 10). History tells us that for the first 300 years of Church history, the vast majority of Christians refused to participate in military service or even hold government positions. In fact, there is no evidence of *a single Christian soldier* after New Testament times until about A.D. 170. [26] The problem with arguments from silence is they can go either way. All we really know from these passages is that Jesus and the Apostles gave

---

26 *War: Four Christian Views* (Intervarsity Press, 1981), 12

people space to figure out for themselves the implications of what it means to live a kingdom lifestyle.

As long as we're arguing from silence then the burden of proof is either on those who advocate violence or on those who renounce violence. As far as I know the only passages in the New Testament that deal directly with how Christians are supposed to relate to those who have harmed them in the past or seek to harm them in the future are Matthew 5:38–48, Luke 6:29, 32, 35, Romans 12:17–21, I Thessalonians 5:15, and I Peter 2:18–23, 3:9. Each and every one of these passages agree that Christians are supposed to love and bless their enemies, turn the other cheek, not repay evil for evil, and are not to avenge themselves, but to leave vengeance to God. Since the New Testament repeatedly teaches that Kingdom of God citizens are supposed to imitate Jesus, and we know that Jesus categorically refused violence at every opportunity, then why should the burden of proof be on Christians who renounce violence and not on Christians who advocate violence?

CHAPTER 7

How Shall We Then Fight?

One of the greatest insults to the Lord Jesus Christ is when His followers try to domesticate the cross. Out of all the ways a human being can pass from this world to the next, crucifixion is arguably the most hideous method ever devised by humans to take a life. The Romans used crucifixion as a way of instilling fear in the hearts and minds of all who would dare oppose her rule and yet, when Jesus says, "Whoever comes after me must deny himself, take up his cross and follow me," we think He's talking about lust, smoking, back aches, and annoying in-laws. It shouldn't come as a surprise to say that the Romans didn't crucify Jesus because they wanted to help 21st century evangelical Christians in their daily devotions. The Romans crucified Jesus because they perceived Him as a threat to their power. Jesus was put to death because He exposed the invalidity of the powers that be of His day and the moral pretext behind their power.

When Jesus said, "Take up your cross and follow me," His audience would have understood Him to be saying, "The powers that be see me as a threat and if you follow me, they're going to see you as a threat too." As a charismatic Christian, I find Jesus' words here puzzling. I can remember growing up thinking that evangelical Christians such as myself are a persecuted minority living in a political culture hostile to Christian values (which I always assumed to be Republican values). Those days are long gone. With the two-time election of George W. Bush to the White House and the discovery of the immensely large voting block known as "values voters", a virtual synonym for "evangelical voters", I witnessed the status of my people go from the underdog to the top dog—with the ability to wage war (literally and metaphorically) like never before. The question American evangelicals now have to ask is how can we be considered a threat to the powerful when we are the powerful?

If Christians are under a divine mandate to seize the reigns of political power, then Jesus used some strange words to characterize His followers' place in the world. Jesus said that His followers would be "harmless as doves" and "like sheep among wolves" (Matthew 10:16). A lamb is utterly defenseless in the face of a raving wolf and a dove—well—it's harmless. Here's the problem. Can anyone be considered harmless as a dove or as an innocent defenseless sheep when he (or she) campaigns for the position of the commander and chief of the world's most powerful military? Is it even possible to imagine Jesus saying something like:

"I would never want to sacrifice one particle of America's power. Ronald Reagan had it right when he led this country to unprecedented military strength. Our best defense is a military so well equipped and so well trained that no one wants to challenge it.

Strength is a far more effective deterrent to war than is weakness, and the US should never be apologetic for the development of the strongest military forces on the face of the earth." [27]

If we replace the word "America" with "Rome," it becomes even more difficult to imagine Jesus uttering a statement such as this. It seems to me that regardless of whether one agrees with this particular statement or not, aspiring to lead and develop the strongest military forces on the face of the earth is a strange way for a follower of Jesus to live out the calling to be a harmless dove or a defenseless lamb. My point here isn't to pick on Mike Huckabee, the governor of Arkansas that uttered this statement while campaigning for the Republican nomination for the presidency in 2007. I have no doubt that Huckabee is a sincere Christian who loves the Lord, but nevertheless I have to ask the question of whether a Christian who confesses Jesus Christ as Lord should aspire to such a lofty position of sword-wielding power—especially when Jesus consistently refused the same type of power throughout His earthly ministry.

A good number of Christians within the Anabaptist tradition (today's Mennonites, Amish, and Church of the Brethren) answer this question by refusing government positions that require them to wield the power of the sword. While I think the majority of Christians today would find this position extreme, I have to admit that I have a lot of respect for this position, not only for the fact that it's the position the vast majority of Christians took for the

27 http://www.ontheissues.org/2008/Mike_Huckabee_Homeland_Security.htm
Accessed July 18th, 2008

first 300 years of church history, but also because the arguments for this position are Biblically sound.

Not withstanding the reasons we've mentioned so far, the New Testament repeatedly teaches that Christians are supposed to be separate from the world (John 15:19, Romans 12:2, 2 Corinthians 6:17, Galatians 1:4, James 1:27). The New Testament also identifies earthly governments with "the kingdoms of this world" (Matthew 4:8, Revelation 11:15). If the one thing that distinguishes Christ's Kingdom from worldly kingdoms is that servants in Christ's Kingdom don't fight, then it shouldn't be thought of as a stretch to ask the question: Can Christians who hold positions of sword-wielding power say in any meaningful sense that they're separate from the world—when they're running the kingdoms of this world's institutions?

Some argue that a withdrawal from worldly affairs amounts to a cowardly cop-out, leaving others to do the dirty work of defending life and liberty while benefiting from other people's sacrifice. This is perhaps the argument with the strongest emotional force when it comes to arguing for a Christian's participation in war, be it as a soldier, a politician, or a voter. The problem with the argument is it reflects a worldly perspective and not a Christian one. The argument assumes that it's man that controls the outcome of history and not God. And yet, over and over throughout Scripture, we see that it's *God* who determines the outcome of battles and *God* who established the nations' borders. Sometimes He sees fit to allow evil rulers to conquer nations more righteous than they, other times He sees fit to allow the righteous to rule. So the question of whether a Christian should participate in war or wield the power of the sword in any way should be determined by what God says about the issue, not by some humanly constructed notion of cause and effect that excludes God's sovereignty.

Notice how no one uses this argument against Mother Theresa or New York City firemen. Nobody says that Mother Theresa was a coward because she chose to spend her life among the poor in Calcutta and not as a military nurse. Neither does anyone question the bravery of a New York City fireman that never serves in the military. The reason is because all of us recognize that the Sisters of Charity and New York City firemen perform a valuable service to society because of their vocations. The same is true for the priests and Levites in the Old Testament. I've heard lots of sermons about the cowardly lion, but never a sermon about the cowardly Levites. That's because every serious student of Scripture knows that the priests and Levites declined from participating in Israel's battles not because of cowardice, but because of obedience to their vocation. So the question that Christians need to ask today is: does the unique vocation of the Church preclude Christians from participating in the taking of another human life—be it through the ballot box, governmental office, or as a soldier in combat?

On the question of whether a Christian should vote or hold public office, I'm pleading the fifth not because I don't think there's merit to the argument that Christians should preserve the purity of the Church as an agent of grace, but because the Bible says, "The letter kills, but the Spirit gives life," (2 Corinthians 3:6). Legalism is always something we need to avoid especially when there's such a wide range of options to choose from (like voting but not holding public office or holding public office but not high office). Having said that, if we ask the question of whether the unique vocation of the Church precludes Christians from fighting in wars for the sake of national interest, I believe there are several factors we need to consider.

One of these factors is the New Testament repeatedly identifies Christ with His Body. What one does to a member of Christ's Body is the same as doing it to Christ Himself (Acts 9:4, I Corinthians 8:12, Ephesians 5:30). At the very least this means that the spiritual unity among members of Christ's Body transcends national boundaries and therefore should trump national interests. If one of the ways the world is supposed to be able to distinguish true disciples from false disciples is that true disciples demonstrate love for the brethren (John 13:35, I John 3:14), then what does this say for Christians killing other Christians simply because some guy (or gal) that lives in a White House says it's in their nation's interests to do so?

Think about it for a moment. Our Pastors unequivocally blessed our American Christian soldiers as they marched off to war, praying for their success in battle. Somehow I wonder if the same pastors who prayed for the success of our American troops would have been willing to pray a similar prayer had they been standing in an Iraqi cathedral crowded with hundreds of frightened Iraqi Christians (Iraq has a sizable Christian minority) on the eve of the invasion? Do we know how many innocent civilians that died during the "shock and awe" bombing campaign were our brothers and sisters in Christ? Or what about Iraqi pastors blessing their Iraqi church members in the Iraqi national army? What would we think if we heard about Iraqi pastors blessing Iraqi soldiers and praying for their success in killing American soldiers? How is it that American Christian leaders spend days on their knees in fasting and prayer for unity in the Body of Christ and then think nothing of killing another member of the Body of Christ simply because their nation's political leaders deem it to be in their best interests?

Another factor to consider is we know that God has entrusted the Church with the vocation of calling people everywhere to repentance and salvation, but have we factored this into the equation of whether it's acceptable for a Christian to participate in the taking of a human life? The Bible says, "It is appointed unto men to die once, but after this the judgment" (Hebrews 9:27). No one is guaranteed a second chance in the afterlife. The only way for anyone to assure salvation from eternal judgment is to place his or her faith in Jesus Christ in this life. This point shouldn't be underestimated because if the chief task of the Church is to preach the gospel so that those who hear can believe and be saved (Romans 10:14), it presents a challenge for someone to hear and believe when they've been killed by a U.S. cluster bomb.* According to former Secretary of State Madeline Albright, the estimated number of Iraqi civilians killed by

---

* a bomb consisting of a canister that releases many bomblets over a wide area. Bomblets often lie dormant until an innocent civilian (often a child) picks it up and is maimed or killed. Civilian deaths from U.S. cluster bombs are grossly under-reported in the U.S. media.

Coalition forces range anywhere from 30,000–100,000 souls. [28] I wonder if preachers that rallied behind the Iraq war ever considered that their actions would lead to the probability of 30,000–100,00 people facing a potential Christ-less eternity?

I find it odd that one of the principle "Christian" arguments for the Iraq war was that it would pave the way for democracy and therefore open up the door for more Iraqis to hear the gospel. In the months preceding the invasion of Iraq, I'll be the first to admit that I bought into this logic and—I'm ashamed to say—even after the death, the looting, and the destruction of the first two years, never seriously questioned it.

Here's the problem with the argument. The same people who made the argument for invading Iraq for the purpose of opening up the nation to the gospel—knowing that the invasion would lead to inevitable civilian casualties—are the same people who vehemently oppose the crass utilitarianism of those who favor embryonic stem-cell research. The same people who say (rightly in my judgment) that it's wrong to create a life for the purpose of destroying it, even if it will save the lives of potentially thousands more people, are the same people that pronounced holy the plunging of thousands of souls into a potential Christ-less eternity for the sake of the *possibility* that more people would have the freedom to hear the gospel. Never mind the fact that the war has actually increased the persecution of Christians in Iraq. I'm

---

28 *The Mighty and the Almighty: Reflections on America, God and World Affairs* (Harper Collins, 2006), 193

wondering why anti-abortion but pro-war Christians insist on referring to themselves as pro-*life* rather than simply pro-*birth*.

If a similar death toll were to occur in the United States, more than 295,000 lives would have been lost—about a hundred times the number of people killed on 9/11—and that's a ridiculously low estimate! What troubles me is that the vast majority of American Christians—especially in the Pentecostal/charismatic tradition—are so thoroughly indoctrinated in state worship that by the time a young American man turns 18 and joins the military, his faith has become so nationalized that it never occurs to him that there might be a contradiction between obeying the command of Jesus to go into all the world and preach the gospel and dropping 30 pound bombs from the sky on defenseless villages for no other reason than that somebody with the last name Bush—or for that matter, Clinton or Obama—ordered him to do it. There comes a time when we have to follow the directions of our commander and chief Jesus over and against the commander and chief Uncle Sam.

The Apostle Paul told Timothy:

"You therefore must endure hardship as a good soldier of Jesus Christ. No one engaged in warfare entangles himself with the affairs of this life, that he may please him who enlisted him as a soldier." (2 Timothy 2:3–4)

Paul made it clear to Timothy that soldiers of Christ are not to entangle themselves in the affairs of this life, but are to have single-minded devotion to the Lord Jesus Christ as their commander in chief. Not only do state soldiers place their lives at the disposal of their commanders, they also have to entrust *other people's lives* to the discretion of their commanders. I have a tremendous amount of respect for soldiers who display courage in battle (especially those who give their lives to save their fellow soldiers), but nevertheless, if I'm going to place my loyalty to Scripture above what's culturally fashionable, then I have to ask the question: Does the type of devotion that requires a person to place his life (and other people's lives) at the disposal of another human being for the sole purpose of advancing the interests of a nation/state qualify for entanglement in the affairs of this life? Can a Christian place their lives in the hands of two separate commander and chiefs—remember that Jesus is the *only* Lord and the *only* Potentate (words that could easily be substituted for the word President today)—without becoming a spiritual schizophrenic?

Another passage we need to consider as we ponder the question of whether a Christian should fight to defend land and liberty is 1 Corinthians 6:1–7 where the Apostle Paul criticized his fellow Corinthian believers for suing each other in a secular court of law. According to Paul, a Christian going to court against another Christian in order to rectify a wrong represents an "utter failure" on the part of the Christian plaintiff. On the surface, it appears this passage has little to say on the participation of a Christian in state-sanctioned wars, but if we probe a little deeper, we'll discover that Paul had an entirely different view of earthly possessions than the average Christian has today.

Amazingly, Paul says it's better to "accept wrong" and to "let yourself be cheated" than for a Christian to seek redress for earthly possessions before unbelievers. What Paul is saying here flies in the face of human nature, especially human nature as represented in classic American culture. Off the top of my head, I can't think of a single American—and that includes American Christians—that would admire someone who let himself be cheated. We think that someone who refuses to "stand up for himself"—whether by defending his life, his personal property, or his land—is weak. New Testament Christians on the other hand esteemed earthly things lightly and "joyfully accepted the plundering of their goods" (Hebrews 10:34). Rather than viewing possessions as something to be fought over and defended, they sold their possessions and shared their wealth with the rest of the Christian community (Acts 2:44–45). They viewed land and possessions as something to be used for the benefit of all, not as something to be grasped onto solely for one's personal benefit. This is why Paul was so ticked off at the Christian plaintiffs in the Corinthian Church. It wasn't just because he was concerned about public relations. It's because he wanted the Corinthian believers to esteem earthly things lightly.

What does this have to do with Christians fighting in wars? Think about it for a moment. If the Apostle Paul didn't approve of Christians *suing* to defend earthly possessions, what makes us think he would approve of Christians *killing* to defend earthly possessions? Even wars fought under the banner of self-defense are typically waged for the purpose of defending land and resources and yet, according to Scripture, New Testament believers are supposed to be "strangers" and "pilgrims" on the earth (Hebrews 11:13). When a man fights for his nation, he's not just fighting to defend *other people's* possessions. He's fighting to defend *his own* possessions. Few (if any) wars are fought purely for the interests of others. Wars are usually (if not always) fought for national interests. Within the *we* of fighting for our nation, there's always the *I* of I'm fighting to protect *my* land, *my* possessions, *my* freedom. And yet land, possessions—and yes, even freedom—are the very things that Christians are supposed to surrender to Christ at the foot of the cross.

Some argue that Christians shouldn't fight to defend themselves, but are morally obligated to take up arms to defend the innocent against an evil aggressor. Given that Saddam Hussein was such a ruthless and brutal dictator, this became the chief justification for the invasion of Iraq for many Christians that I know. Let me say first that I have a *lot* of respect for this position. When I think about the senseless slaughter of Tutsis in Rwanda, Jews during the holocaust, and the ethnic cleansing taking place in Darfur today, I find it very difficult to challenge the idea that a Christian isn't morally justified to take up arms to defend the innocent against the wicked. Having said that, I remain unconvinced that it's the proper place for a Christian to bear the sword even in extreme situations.

If there ever was a time when it would have been justified to use the sword to defend the innocent, it would have been when Peter used the sword to defend Jesus from a cruel and torturous crucifixion, but amazingly, Jesus *rebuked* Peter for using the sword *even then.* Some say that the only reason Jesus stopped Peter is because He knew He had to go to the cross to die for the sins of the world, but notice that Jesus did *not* say, "I appreciate the thought Peter, but I'm doing this for the sins of the world, so save your sword for another occasion." Instead He said, "Put your sword in its place, for *all* who take the sword will perish by the sword," (italics emphasis mine). The question is simple. Is Jesus our moral example or is He not?

I don't buy the argument that the U.S. invaded Iraq to save innocent Iraqis from the clutches of a cruel dictator, but even if this were the case, I'd still have to challenge it on biblical grounds. In Acts 17:26, Paul tells the Athenians in his famous Mars Hill message that God, "has made from one blood every nation of men to dwell on the face of the earth, and has determined their preappointed times and the boundaries of their dwellings." If it's God that determines nation's borders, then it stands to reason that no nation has the authority to invade another nation, even if the purpose is promoting "freedom" and "democracy." And for all my Christian friends that believe it's their duty to submit the U.S. government to Biblical standards, if the U.S. government *really* wanted to go by the book, then our nation wouldn't have had a standing army by which we could have attacked Saddam in the first place! (Deuteronomy 17:16)

Our nations TV preachers are hell bent on attacking Iran's nuclear facilities with tactical nuclear weapons, something that would with *100 percent certainty*, result not only in massive civilian casualties (a good number of them being recent converts to

Christianity), but would also have catastrophic consequences on the land itself. I wonder if the same TV preachers have ever read Deuteronomy 20:19 where God forbade the children of Israel from destroying their enemy's trees because the tree is used for man's food. If God forbade Israel from destroying its enemies *trees*, then what makes us think He would approve of weapons that have the potential of destroying *much more than* trees? If these same rich suburban mega-church preachers were really as concerned about restoring Biblical righteousness to our nation's government, they would be on the front lines of the nuclear disarmament movement, and, by all means they'd be urging the U.S. to ban the use of landmines.

At least in my short lifetime of 30 years, the denouncing of any projection of American military might has *always* been the quickest way to land a charismatic Christian in the loony bin among his or her peers. The same leaders that insist they're God's defenders of life, liberty, and the pursuit of happiness spend hours on their knees in prayer that God will send us another leader like Ronald Reagan—the same leader that supported the death squads in El Salvador, invaded Grenada, conducted a terrorist campaign in Nicaragua, supported the training of Latin American dictators to torture their political opponents in the famous School of Americas, and was the principle actor in the Iron/Contra scandal.

Again, my point isn't to single out Ronald Reagan. Nearly every U.S. president has supported human rights abuses in the name of national interest—including Bill Clinton. For better or worse, that's what political leaders do. But for all of the moral posturing that goes on in the name of "taking America back for God", is it really that difficult to imagine why some on the outside accuse us of hypocrisy when we declare ourselves the "moral majority" simply because we like guns and babies—but don't like gays— and then we turn around and demonize those who think that it's wrong for a nation to back dictators who slaughter and torture their people? I wonder if Jesus were around today if He'd accuse our leaders of straining gnats and swallowing camels the same way He accused the Pharisees of His day. Worse yet, I wonder if the words "brood of vipers" would enter His vocabulary.

Readers are sure to pick up allusions to hot-button issues on the conservative political agenda in the above paragraph. Abortion. Gay marriage. Gun rights. My point isn't to pinpoint the "Christian" perspective on any of them. Neither is it my intention to demonize the evangelical right. A family member the other day asked me, "So when did you become a left-wing ideologue?" Given my anti-war position and my refusal to absolutize certain political issues as litmus tests to determine whether a person can be termed "one of us" or not, I can certainly understand the question, though I think the question is misdirected. The question assumes that Christian values can be translated into the political sphere in cookie cutter black and white fashion without considerable shades of grey in between. Scripture clearly teaches that God's people are not to put their trust in princes (Psalms 146:3) and, yet, too often we in the evangelical world look to politicians (as long as they're on *our* side of certain issues) to save us from our nations woes. We see the abortions, the homosexuality, immorality run rife, and we feel that we can vote away our problems with a magic wand—as if declaring abortion illegal will actually stop abortions from taking place and banning gay marriage will actually stop homosexuals from engaging in gay sex.

Might I suggest another way? The Bible says, "For the weapons of our warfare are not carnal but mighty in God for pulling down strongholds" (II Corinthians 10:4). It must be the result of some pretty severe cultural conditioning that the average American Christian doesn't see this verse as a slight against the use of physical weapons to achieve moral ends. Using physical weapons to achieve desired ends is the way the world operates, but not the way Christians are supposed to operate. The problem with Christians lobbying Caesar to legislate morality is that Caesar relies on force to keep himself in power, and this is true whether Caesar is a dictator or whether Caesar is a democracy. All governments rely on the power of the sword to control their population's behavior. Whether the sword is used for righteous purposes or unrighteous purposes, the sword is still the sword. Both Jesus and Paul refused the power of the sword *even to achieve moral ends*. Were they crazy or is it because they believed in a better way? If we don't fight with weapons, how shall we then fight?

I'm going to go out on a limb here, but I believe that in the end, there are no political solutions to the world's problems. The only real hope for the world lies not in politics, but in the Church. God has entrusted His Church with the twin weapons of preaching the gospel and prayer and it's only because of our succumbing to modernism that we don't think that's enough. Allow me to further go out on a limb and say that I don't believe it's the Church's job to solve the world's problems. The job of the Church is to imitate Calvary, and only by imitating Calvary can we effect any real and lasting change in the world, and even *then*, change is never the aim, only the byproduct.

As tempting as it might be to prefer pimping Caesar at the ballot box over the way of Calvary that calls us to sacrifice our lives for the sake of others, let's not give the world a cheap substitute for authentic discipleship. The way of Calvary says that Christians that want to save babies should be the first in line to sacrifice their financial futures to help unwed mothers. The way of Calvary says that Christians that want to fight the War on Terror should be giving generously to bless Iran with Bibles, not bombs. Jesus said, "Greater love has no man than this, than one lays down his life for his friends."

On the homepage of Christian Peacemaker Teams, an organization dedicated to reducing violent conflict around the world, are the words, "What would happen if Christians devoted the same discipline and self-sacrifice to nonviolent peacemaking that armies devote to war?" [29] The alternative to engaging in state-sanctioned violence is laying down our arms and picking up the cross.

---

29 http://www.cpt.org Accessed July 18th, 2008

CHAPTER 8

Ethnic Cleansing for Jesus

Nearly a year after my debate with Khalid, I participated in a delegation to the West Bank with an organization called Christian Peacemaker Teams. Growing up in a charismatic Mega church and having attended one of the most pro-Israel Bible colleges in the nation, the only reference I had up until my encounter with Khalid was that of an individual thoroughly schooled in the viewpoint of Christian Zionism. In a nutshell, Christian Zionism teaches that due to God's promise to Abraham in Genesis 12:1–3, Christians are obligated to support the modern nation/state of Israel. Some go as far as to actively finance Jewish settlements in the West Bank. Others are less enthusiastic about getting involved in the political side of things, but still live with the underlying assumption that any word or action that even so much as hints at questioning the projection of Israeli military power or the God-given right of Jews to expand their borders is sure to incur the wrath of God. Most people that I know in the

Pentecostal/charismatic movement fall into the second category, even if their assumptions are largely unknown to them.

Knowing that some of my friends were concerned about me putting myself on God's naughty list because I was traveling to Israel to learn about the conflict from the Palestinian point of view, I made sure that I asked all the tough questions. Every time the group met with a journalist or a human rights worker, with an Israeli peace activist or a Palestinian farmer, I made sure that the delegation didn't leave without me grueling the speaker with every question or possible objection that could be raised from the other side. I'm reasonably certain that I drove the rest of the delegation nuts in the process, but I couldn't return home without knowing that I had made every possible attempt to be objective.

Since I've returned home, I've communicated what I saw to many of my friends and family and as much as I've tried, I'm just not sure how to talk about the day to day suffering of ordinary Palestinians living in East Jerusalem, the West Bank, and the Gaza Strip without running the risk of being labeled an anti-Semite, a heretic, one-sided, or just plain naïve. Worse yet, how do I communicate what I've seen without actually *becoming* those things? Since the issues are still raw for me at this point, I've decided to focus on the stories of people I met on my journey.

First, let me tell you about Fadi. Fadi is a Palestinian Christian living in Bethlehem. Fadi is the associate pastor of a charismatic church and teaches at Bethlehem Bible College. When Fadi took a group of Palestinian Christians to a conference in Korea, it took the group 12 hours to get to Amman, Jordan (a trip that should only take 1 hour). Because Fadi and the group were Palestinians, they had to pass through a check point to leave Bethlehem, a checkpoint to enter Jericho, and when the group reached the border to Jordan, they had to cross a Palestinian checkpoint, two Israeli checkpoints, and, finally, the Jordanian checkpoint. If Fadi wants to go to East Jerusalem, he has to apply for a permit, which he may or may not get, and, if he does, he may only be allowed into the city for 5–7 hours. Those who are fortunate enough to get permits to work in East Jerusalem, must get up at 3:30 a.m. in order to get to their work-place (which is only 8 miles away) by 7:30 a.m. The reason for this is because of a massive wall built by the Israeli military that now surrounds Bethlehem.

I can hear the half screams already. "But Aaron! Don't you realize that the wall is there to protect innocent Jews from suicide bombers?" Well, that's not how the Palestinians see it. They see it as a land grab. A significant number of Israeli Jews also see it that way. First of all, as one Israeli Jew pointed out to me, walls haven't been a significant means of protecting cities since about the middle ages. With the advent of modern technology, desperate people can always dig tunnels and even more desperate people can launch rockets, as we've seen people living in the Gaza strip do. More importantly, the wall, which the Israelis call a "security fence," isn't built around the internationally recognized border separating the state of Israel from the occupied territories (which is called the Green Line).

Nobody in their right mind would morally object to a nation defending its borders. The problem is the wall cuts into the heart of the West Bank, dividing people from their families, separating people from their farmlands, and, in many cases, cutting people off from any significant means of survival—all without compensation. In some cases, the wall actually surrounds people's homes so that when they look out their windows, there's a concrete wall staring back at them over twice the size of the house and surrounding them on all three sides. I met one Palestinian family (a Christian family) who had a thriving business out of their garage on a very busy street, but now the wall surrounds their home like a prison.

To add insult to injury, in many cases, the wall is strategically placed on private property owned by Palestinian farmers, cutting the farmers off from their fields and leaving ample room for the Jew-only settlements to expand. In some cases, the wall even surrounds entire villages, making further room for settlement expansions. What should further alarm us about the settlements and the wall that protects them is not only do the settlements divert a disproportionate amount of the water resources away from the Palestinians, I also heard many stories of the settlements, which are nearly all sitting on top of hills adjacent to Palestinian villages, dumping their sewage onto the hillsides. After dumping their sewage on their neighbors, settlers use the walls to isolate themselves from their neighbors. As one Palestinian Christian man put it sadly to me, "They don't even want to see our faces."

After the Jewish settlements are well established and the Palestinian people have no hope of farming their land again, the IDF (the Israeli Defense Force) then builds roads to connect the settlements, roads that are for Israelis only. In many cases, if a home is in the way or anywhere near the road, it's simply demolished (again without compensation). Such was the case with Atta, a Palestinian tomato farmer whose home I stayed in for a night. Atta's home has already been demolished twice and the home he is living in currently is his third home. If Atta and his family leave the house for any lengthy period of time, they face the risk of armed Jewish settlers seizing the house and claiming it for God. The part about Atta's story that should give us all hope is the fact that both times his home has been demolished Jewish peace activists have helped him rebuild.

The next places I went to were Susiya and At-Wani. I'm not even sure where to begin when talking about these villages. First, I'll start with the children. Because the children living near At-Wani have to walk between two heavily guarded settlements to get to school, they face the daily threat of attacks from Jewish settlers. In the past, the elementary school children have been harassed and attacked by grown men wearing black masks. Because of this, they have to be escorted to school by Israeli soldiers who often either don't show up or, if they do, will make the journey difficult by going too fast in their jeeps for the children to follow. Though some of the soldiers aren't as bad (some have been known to give the kids candy from time to time), Christian Peacemaker Teams has a daily presence there of monitoring the soldiers to make sure the kids can travel to school safely and without harassment. In addition to monitoring the soldiers, team members carry video cameras with them and watch the shepherds and the farmers who also face daily threats and harassments (and sometimes attacks) by the settlers. The settlers can carry hand pistols. The Palestinian farmers cannot.

As I walked through the villages of Susiya and At-Wani, the stories were very similar. In Susiya, I saw a community of people living in tents. Each and every tent had been demolished more than once and, even though the Israeli high court declared that the land was theirs, they still needed a permit to live on the land. The villagers showed me a cistern that the Israeli Defense Force came and filled with rocks so the people wouldn't be able to access their water supply. A similar occurrence happened in At-Wani when a group of settlers poisoned their water supply with a poison that can only be obtained by a permit. Because of the poisoned water supply, in addition to restricted water access, the people weren't able to sell their sheep that drank from the water, thus crippling the village economy. Because the villagers are living under military occupation, they had no legal recourse and there has never been an investigation to this day. Another troubling fact is how the Israeli military refuses to grant permission to the people to build clinics and schools in their own village without facing the threat of demolition.

After spending time in Susiya and At-Wani, I went to Hebron, a city where over 850 shops have been closed down by a military order, the people have to pass through 101 checkpoints to get to where they need to go, and where just a few short years ago, the people endured a 586 day curfew where they could only come out of their homes once a week for a period of three hours before they had to return to their homes. As I walked through the streets, I noticed several nets hanging above me connecting the buildings on both sides. I also noticed bottles and blocks and numerous other dangerous objects lying on top of the nets. These were areas where the settlers (who are fully protected by the Israeli military) throw things out the windows for the sole purpose of maiming or killing their Palestinian neighbors walking on the streets. Although on paper, the soldiers are supposed to protect the Palestinians as well as the settlers, the reality on the ground tells a different story. In 1994, when a Jewish settler named Baruch Goldstein entered the Abraham mosque (located within the Cave of the Patriarchs) and massacred 29 people, the Israeli military responded by imposing a curfew on the Palestinians (but not the settlers), closing down the city's primary Palestinian vegetable market, and establishing new routes for Jews only to walk between the settlements located in the heart of the city.

How did the settlers arrive in Hebron? The stories I heard were mostly the same regardless of where I went. A Palestinian leaves their home for a few days, a Jewish settler moves in while they are absent, the Israeli military declares their home or apartment a closed military zone, and the individual or family is unable to return. Entire apartment complexes are seized this way and when the process is complete, the Israeli military will shut down a street, force the people out of their homes or shops, and declare it a street for Jews only. What is absolutely mind-boggling to me is the fact that there are Christians in America supporting some of these settlers financially.

In Hebron I met many fascinating people, including two Palestinian journalists who told stories of Palestinian human rights activists being arrested without charges and enduring torture in Israeli prisons. The journalists themselves showed scars on their bodies from the beatings they had endured from Israeli soldiers in the past. The journalists also told us about the plight of hundreds of women and children locked away in Israeli prisons. While most of us think of Palestinian prisoners as terrorists, some are in prison simply for resisting a land confiscation or a home demolition. Nearly all are held indefinitely without a trial. I also met with local Palestinian police who were struggling to maintain order among their people despite the obstacles the Israeli military put in their way (like letting a thief get away and not allowing the police to pass through the checkpoints).

One of the most inspiring people I met in Hebron was Zleika. Zleika is a schoolteacher who courageously defied the curfew imposed by the IDF, often going out during the day and forming a line to take her students to school. Zleika told us about a day she was passing through a checkpoint holding a sack of sweet potatoes in her hands when a female soldier made the comment "garbage holding garbage." When the soldier asked her what was in the bag, Zleika replied, "That is my business, not yours." The soldier responded by pushing Zleika to the ground and beating her repeatedly while the other soldiers did nothing. After Zleika got up, the other soldiers joined in by throwing her to the ground, strip-searching her twice, and, when the incident was over, they took her to the police where Zleika was questioned for 10 hours. The female soldier claimed that Zleika beat her up. The police told her that if the case went to court, she would have to pay 1,000 shekels (roughly 250 dollars, equivalent to 3 months wages). As terrible as the story is, was this an isolated incident? No. Another time Zleika was beaten by a group of soldiers for protecting a young boy they were harassing. After hearing Zleika's story, and other stories like hers, I couldn't help but imagine what the long term prospects of peace were if the only Jews that Palestinian children ever see are those behind the barrel of a gun.

Through meeting with groups like ACRI (the Association of Civil Rights in Israel), the UNRWA (the United Nations Relief Workers Agency), and even the Palestinian YMCA, I learned about many of the numerical facts on the ground. For example, in the past 7 years the Israeli army has uprooted over 466,000 olive trees mostly to make room for new Jew-only settlements. Many of these olive trees are over 2,000 years old and are considered heirlooms by their owners. A significant amount of Palestinians also rely on these olive trees to feed their families. In addition to the olive trees that have been destroyed, the Israeli army has destroyed 1.4 million trees and thousands of acres of farmland in the Palestinian territories since September of 2,000.

And that's just in the Palestinian territories. I also learned from ACRI, which is a civil rights organization in Israel, that despite what I've been told about how wonderful Arab-Israelis have it in

Israel, there exists today severe discrimination against Arab Israelis, especially when it comes to property rights—the hallmark of any true democracy. According to ACRI, since the establishment of the State of Israel, not one Arab city has been established (with the exception of seven Bedouin townships built on land owned by Bedouin tribes), even though the Arab population has grown seven-fold. In the same period, 600 Jewish communities have been established throughout Israel. In order to end this policy of land and housing discrimination, ACRI raises awareness among their fellow Israeli citizens by producing videos that portray the heart-wrenching personal stories of Arab citizens who have been unable to build homes on their own land because of this discriminatory policy. What may come as a surprise to Christians in the States is ACRI is largely a Jewish-led organization. Not all Jews are Zionists— even in Israel.

I also learned that in 1948, the year Israel became a nation, approximately 800,000 Palestinians were driven from their homes. Many of them were forced out at gunpoint, others left out of fear. During this time, children were slaughtered, women were raped, houses were burned to the ground, land mines were planted, and Israeli tanks shelled entire villages. Overall 531 villages were destroyed. Those who fled for their lives have not been allowed to return to their homes till this day even though international law mandates their right of return and most of the villages remain vacant to this day. I realize there are many who claim that the Palestinians woke up one day and decided to join a massive Arab army to drive Jews into the sea, and that's how the refugee problem was created. The problem with this idea is if you listen to the refugees, they tell a completely different story, and even some of Israel's top historians are calling the events surrounding the formation of Israel ethnic cleansing. [30]

There's no question in my mind that the events surrounding the formation of Israel are fraught with moral ambiguity. Consider that May 15th, 1948 is celebrated as Independence Day in Israel (much like Americans celebrate the 4th of July) while the same day is considered a day of mourning among the Palestinians. Palestinians refer to the day as the Nakba, a word that means catastrophe in Arabic. Between the Israeli version and the Palestinian version of what happened in 1948, I'm sure the truth is somewhere in the middle. But it's the very fact that the truth is so complex and rife with moral difficulty that I can't help but marvel at all the books and articles I've read over the years, from some of the most respected American evangelical leaders of my time, that declare the events of 1948 a divine miracle. Not just a miracle, but also an answer to prayer. I've seen numerous newsletters from revival organizations that look back to the formation of Israel as an answer to prayer and use it as an example of what can happen if Americans would pray for revival today. Am I missing something or am I out of my mind

---

30 The most notable Israeli historian that refer to the events surrounding the formation of is Ilan Pappe. Ilan Pappe's book *The Ethnic Cleansing of Palestine* describes this time period in fascinating detail.

because I can't figure out why I'm supposed to equate an outpouring of the Holy Spirit with massacre and destruction?

Another thing that surprised me was how many of the refugees I met that actually preferred a one state solution to the conflict over a two state solution. Though it's been 60 years, the families I met showed me deeds to their homes that date back to the Ottoman empire and nearly all of them said that all they wanted was to return to Israel and rebuild their homes and villages (which most of them remain unoccupied to this day with the exception for a third of them which were taken over by Jews). According to one intellectual I met, over 65% of the Palestinian elite want a *secular* democracy—not an Islamic state—with equal rights for Jews and Palestinians alike. Their attitude is that if Jews can build towns in the West Bank, then they should be able to live in Haifa or Tel Aviv. This shows me that, despite the propaganda, the majority of Palestinians are willing to live with Jews, as long as they aren't discriminated against by a system aimed at preserving a racial majority for Jews. For many Palestinians, this would mean equality. For Zionists, of course, this would mean the destruction of Israel.

By far the person that made the greatest impression on me was a young man named Gilad. Gilad is an Israeli Jew who works with an organization called ICAHD, which stands for Israeli Committee Against Home Demolitions. After Gilad graduated from high school, he refused to serve the mandatory two years in the army for reasons of conscience. Though he's been culturally ostracized from many of his friends and family for refusing to join the IDF, Gilad works to rebuild Palestinian homes that have been demolished by the IDF. Before taking the delegation on a tour of East and West Jerusalem, Gilad gave a lecture on how traditionally the Israeli/Palestinian issue has been viewed from the prism of Israeli security verses Palestinian terrorism. Gilad wanted the team to rethink the issue in light of human rights and international law.

One of the terms Gilad repeatedly emphasized is "the matrix of control" a term used to describe all the different ways in which the Israeli government maintains their dominion over the Palestinian people. In addition to talking about the home demolitions, Gilad talked about land seizures, curfews, the disproportionate use of force aimed at the civilian population, road closures, the concrete blocks the IDF puts in front of Palestinian villages to restrict commerce, checkpoints, travel restrictions, the permit system, the diversion of the water resources and the cutting off of electricity. All of these form what Gilad called the matrix of control.

As Gilad gave the delegation a bus tour of East and West Jerusalem, he instructed us to pay attention to the differences in living conditions between West Jerusalem and East Jerusalem. Every year, approximately 100 Palestinian homes are demolished in East Jerusalem. The people wake up in the morning with an eviction notice. They're given two hours to pack up and leave. After their home is demolished, the IDF hands the family a bill to pay for the demolition. The official government policy to support this practice is called "Judaization," preserving the Jewish majority. According to ICAHD's website, since 1967, over 18,000 homes have been demolished. [31] Only 5% were declared to be for security reasons. Not only does this take place in East Jerusalem, it also takes place elsewhere inside the state of Israel. Every year, entire Bedouin villages are leveled in the Negev valley. The Israeli government justifies this by saying the Bedouins are squatters, squatters in a land they and their ancestors have lived for thousands of years.

The Bible says in Proverbs 18:17, "The first one to plead his cause seems right until his neighbor comes and examines him." Like many of my friends and family, I grew up only hearing one side of this story. Since I've returned from my trip to the West Bank and begun sharing what I saw with other Christians, the most common response I've gotten is *I had no idea that was going on over there.* Most people then ask me, *why haven't I heard this side of the story before?* I usually balk at this question because whichever way I answer it, I'll either sound fanatical or I'll have to shake somebody's worldview. I could say the Pro-Israel lobby (particularly AIPAC) is the most powerful lobby in the world and doesn't want the American public to know the truth about the lives of ordinary Palestinians living in the Occupied territories, but then I remember Mel Gibson's alleged comment about Jews controlling the media. *Scratch off that one!* Or I could say that maybe you haven't heard this side because the only people you've ever listened to about this issue are your favorite radio

---

31 http://www.icahd.org/eng/faq.asp?menu=9&submenu=1
Accessed July 18th, 2008

and TV preachers, but do I really want to tell Sweet Sister Sally that her spiritual leaders are leading her to accept a worldview that says racism, colonialism, and violence are okay as long as it's Arabs that are affected and not Jews? How do I tell Sweet Sister Sally these things without damaging her faith?

Another common response I get is "Wait a minute Aaron. You're only presenting one side. Certainly you know there are two sides to every story." To this I usually reply, "Exactly! There *are* two sides to every story, but let me ask you this. When was the last time you saw a story on the news about Jewish peace activists working along-side Palestinian human rights organizations to protest a home demolition or a land confiscation? These things take place every single week and we hardly ever hear about it in the U.S. media, and you're trying to tell me the U.S. media is biased in favor of Palestinians? Furthermore, did you even know that Palestinian human rights organizations dedicated to non-violence exist, and that not only do they exist but many of them train their fellow Palestinians every single year in methods of non-violent peaceful resistance? Lastly, why do you apply the two-sides argument only to one side? Are you really interested in hearing both sides are do you only get upset when *your* particular side is challenged?"

For the record, I do understand there are two sides to this story. I understand that both sides have committed awful atrocities against each other. But the key word here is both, not just one. I also understand that Israelis have a genuine fear for their security and, of course, all acts of violence targeting civilians should be condemned. I believe that Israel has the right to exist in safe and secure borders. I also know that, contrary to Christian Zionist propaganda, the majority of Palestinians—and indeed the Arab world—also see the recognition of Israel's right to exist as a key element of any successful peace agreement. [32]

Unlike what some Christians believe, I don't believe it's impossible for Jews and Arabs to live at peace just because Jews have the Bible and Muslims have the Koran. Before the dawning of the 20th century, Jews living in the Middle East lived in relative peace with Arabs for centuries. As a matter of historical fact, Jews living in Arab communities fared much better than Jews living in "Christian" Europe during the periods of the Middle Ages and the Inquisition. Yes it's true that both sides have committed awful atrocities against each other, but look at Serbs and Bosnians. They committed awful atrocities against each other as well and now they're living in relative peace with each other. If Christian Serbs and Bosnian Muslims can find a way to work out their differences, then why can't Israelis and Palestinians? What if Jimmy Carter had shared the same worldview when he was president, the worldview that says conflict is inevitable in the Middle East because Jews are sons of Isaac and Arabs are sons of Ishmael? If Carter had believed that while he was president, then Israel and Egypt would still be launching rockets at each other to this day.

I find it odd that Christian Zionists leaders have unabashedly denounced Carter as anti-Semitic, a heretic, and an enemy of

---

32 For a detailed look at the conflict from both sides, read Jimmy Carter's book *Palestine: Peace not Apartheid* (Simon and Schuster, 2006)

Israel just because he dared to compare the situation in the West Bank and the Gaza strip to Apartheid (a comparison that South African leaders like Nelson Mandela and Bishop Desmond Tutu accept by the way) and yet who is the one president who has actually persuaded an Arab nation to stop launching attacks into Israel? Why is it that Christian Zionist leaders who claim to "bless Israel" vilify the one man who has saved more Jewish lives in Israel than all of them combined? Furthermore, why isn't this obvious to everyone? Could it be that American Christians reared on Hal Lindsay's *The Late Great Planet Earth* need to build an alternative worldview?

Herein lies the problem. When I ask a typical educated but non-religious American this question, they'll say the answer is obviously yes. When I ask the typical mega-church evangelical this question, they look at me like I've just arrived from another planet. Over the past few years, I've learned that many secular Americans (and, ironically, a number of Jews) who try to reason with left-behind-theology Christians share the same frustration. They put us in the same class as alien chasers and Kool-Aid drinkers. They can't understand why Christians who claim they follow the Prince of Peace are so hell-bent on keeping the conflict going in the Middle East. A few months back, I was talking with a secular Jew in my city that brings Jews and Arabs together to discuss the Israeli/Palestinian conflict. When I told him about my trip with Christian Peacemaker Teams, he proceeded to tell me, "I don't know if you know this, but many evangelical Christians sponsor Jews to live in Israel because they believe that by preserving a racial majority of Jews in the region, they're hastening the return of Jesus. The odd part about it is, these people also believe that before Jesus comes back, there's going to be a massive war in which $2/3^{rds}$ of the Jews in Israel are going to be slaughtered. Can you believe that? They're literally sending us to our deaths!"

It's one thing for Christians to disagree on things like speaking in tongues, the proper mode of baptism, and the nature of the Trinity. Thankfully, Christians in the West no longer kill each other over these issues like we did in times past. But when it comes to the question of whether or not a Christian should support home demolitions and land confiscations, policies that lead to hatred and resentment and the perpetuation of violent conflict, I wonder why so many in the evangelical camp feel that these are minor issues that should be left alone for the sake of unity? Perhaps the most traumatic question I've ever had to ask myself is "Is it even *possible* to build an alternative worldview from the Scriptures without succumbing to theological relativism?" While the process has been unsettling, the conclusion I've come to is not only is it possible, it's crucial. Leaders like John Hagee and the late Jerry Falwell have declared that Palestinians in the region have to leave to make way for the Jewish people—either voluntarily or by force. Unless we're all willing to walk around with the mark of *Ethnic Cleansing For Jesus* on our foreheads, something has to change—before it's too late.

CHAPTER 9

Debunking the White Elephant

I imagine there are lots of people that would be shocked at the suggestion that much of what goes on in the name of "blessing Israel" is really "ethnic cleansing for Jesus." I hate to be the bearer of bad news, but that's exactly what it is. What else can I call it when I hear leaders like Pat Robertson say that God struck former prime minister Ariel Sharon with a stroke because he withdrew the settlers—remember that the settlements are for Jews *only*—from the Gaza Strip, and then I see high profile politicians follow lock stop and suit just so they can pacify their "evangelical" voter base. As disturbing as that is, it's not the Pat Robertsons and the John Hagees and the Jerry Falwells that upset me the most. At least everyone knows where they stand. It's the tacit approval of "moderate" Christian leaders that I find intolerable. Edmund Burke once said, "The only thing necessary for the triumph of evil is for good men to do nothing."

For the past 60 years, there's been an unholy alliance between a large segment of the evangelical population in the U.S. and far-right extremist groups in Israel. The alliance has but one aim in mind—to preserve a racial majority for the Jewish people in the modern state of Israel and to help the state expand its borders no matter the cost to human lives. If there were a party in the U.S. that had "preserving an Anglo-Saxon majority" as part of it's official platform, we'd call that racism, but the reason why few evangelical leaders are willing to label extreme Zionism with the epithet "racism" is because there's a white elephant in the room, and the elephant's name is Christian Zionism. In my opinion Christian Zionism is the single greatest factor that precludes the vast majority of evangelical Christians, *especially* those in the Pentecostal/charismatic movement, from embracing biblical non-violence. One of the toughest questions I've had to ask myself throughout this amazing spiritual journey is: Can the white elephant of Christian Zionism be debunked or will the word *evangelical* forever be wedded to an ideology of permanent war and dispossession?

It all goes back to Abraham. The Holy Grail verse for Christian Zionists is Genesis 12:3 which says:

"I will bless those who bless you and I will curse him who curses you; And in you all the families of the earth shall be blessed."

Christian Zionists believe this verse applies to modern day-Israel. This is why in the mindset of Christian Zionists, the one thing protecting America from God's judgment for all the evil deeds of gays, feminists, and the Democratic party is America's staunch support of Israel. This one verse in the Bible is repeated so often in Christian Zionists churches that to even entertain the thought that a personal blessing to Abraham might not apply to a nation/state created 4,000 years later is tantamount to blasphemy.

The problem with the Christian Zionist's interpretation of Scripture is that it fails to take into consideration how Jesus and the Apostles interpreted the Old Testament. The assumption Christian Zionists make when interpreting this verse is that the recipients of the promise are the physical descendants of Abraham. The Apostle Paul, however, emphasized in his letter to the Galatians that the promise was made not to Abraham's *seeds*, but to Abraham's *Seed*. According to the Apostle Paul, the recipient of Abraham's promise isn't a people, but a person, and that person is Jesus Christ (Galatians 3:15). Like the other Apostles, Paul saw Israel's story as dramatically fulfilled in the person of Jesus. This is why Paul referred to the Church as "the Israel of God" (Galatians 6:16), because the Church is made up of Jews and Gentiles united by faith to the true Israel—Jesus.

Despite what a few critics claim, the conviction that Jesus is the true Israel isn't an invention of the Apostle Paul, but is shared by the writers of the four gospels as well. For example, in Matthew 2:15, Matthew took a passage in Hosea about God calling Israel out of Egypt and applied it to Christ (Hosea 11:1). In Matthew's mind, everything in the Jesus narrative is a retelling of Israel's narrative. Jesus as the Jewish messiah succeeded at the very point in which national Israel failed, namely to be a light to the nations. Why was Jesus tempted in the wilderness for 40 days and not 39?

The answer is because *Israel* wandered in the desert for 40 years because of their unbelief.

Perhaps the most revolutionary statement Jesus made in His earthly ministry was, "I am the true vine, and my Father is the vinedresser" (John 15:1) This statement must have been a shock to Jesus' disciples because for them, Jews meticulously familiar with the Old Testament, *Israel* was the vine. (See Psalm 80:2, Isaiah 5:2, Jeremiah 2:21, Ezekiel chapters 15 and 17, and Hosea 10:1) By declaring Himself to be the *true* vine, Jesus was essentially telling His Jewish audience, "You think the central character in the story of God's redemptive plan for mankind is you, but really, it's Me."

Unlike what Christian Zionists teach, the Apostles did *not* teach that God has two "peoples" on the earth. In the minds of the apostles, God has always had and always will have only one people. This is crucial to understand because the very foundation of Christian Zionism rests on the idea that God has two different covenants with two different peoples. God's covenant for His earthly people is centered on the land of Israel, the Temple, and the earthly city of Jerusalem while God's covenant with His heavenly people, the Church, centers on the spiritual blessings of a relationship with Christ.

The Apostle Paul begs to differ. In Ephesians 2:14–16 Paul says:

"For He Himself is our peace, who has made *both one* and has broken down the middle wall of separation, having abolished in His flesh the enmity, that is, the law of commandments contained in ordinances, so as to create in Himself *one new man from the two*, thus making peace, and that He might reconcile them both to God *in one body* through the cross," (italics emphasis mine).

Notice that the Apostle Paul says God "has made both *one*" and has created *"one new man from the two."* In Paul's mind, God has only one people. The idea that Jews and Gentiles who form the Church have one covenant with God while unbelieving Jews are under a different covenant is absolutely foreign to Paul's thinking. Unlike before when Gentiles were "aliens from the commonwealth of Israel" and "strangers from the covenants of promise" (Ephesians 2:12) now that Christ has come, God's definition of Israel is no longer racially exclusive, but inclusive. It's not that the Church has *replaced* Israel as the people of God. Rather, the definition of Israel has been expanded to include Gentiles. The two are now one.

The Apostle Peter agrees. Here's what Peter, the same man who "played the hypocrite" with Barnabas by refusing to eat with Gentile believers (see Galatians 2:11–14), wrote to a largely Gentile audience near the end of his life:

"But you are a chosen generation, a royal priesthood, a holy nation, His own special people, that you may proclaim the praises of Him who called you out of darkness into His marvelous light; who once were not a people, but are now the people of God" (I Peter 2:9–10).

Notice that Peter did *not* say to his Gentile audience you are now a people of God. He says you are *the* people of God. Peter did *not* teach that God has two peoples on the earth. In Peter's mind, now that Jesus has arrived on the scene, God has only one people—the Church. Notice that Peter used the words *royal priesthood*, and *holy nation*. Why are these words significant? These are the words used to describe the children of Israel under the Old Covenant (Exodus 19:6). Peter *deliberately* used terms descriptive of ancient Israel and applied them to the Church.

The same can be said for the word *chosen*. In Christian Zionist circles, the idea that ethnic Jews are God's chosen people is about as elementary as the doctrine of the Virgin Birth. The problem with this view is that the New Testament uses the word chosen 29 times and *never once* does it refer exclusively to ethnic Jews. The word *chosen* sometimes refers to Christ (as in Matthew 12:18, Luke 23:35) other times it refers to the Apostles (as in John 13:18 and John 15:16), but more often than not, the word "chosen" is used to describe the Church (see Ephesians 1:4 and I Peter 2:4).

The same pattern emerges with the word *elect*. What's remarkable about the fact that the Apostles used the term *elect* nine different times in the New Testament to describe the Church is the fact that the word Prophet Isaiah used the word *elect* in no uncertain terms to describe national Israel (Isaiah 45:4). The meaning couldn't be clearer. Under the Old Covenant, Israel was God's elect. Under the New Covenant, God's elect is the Church.

I realize that talking about the Church as God's chosen people over and against the idea that religious and ethnic Jews (and modern day Israel) are God's chosen people is an emotionally contentious one, and I can understand why. For centuries, "so called" Christians have persecuted Jews mercilessly often viewing them as inferior, even subhuman. This, of course, must be absolutely condemned. Anti-Semitism is a stench in the nostrils of God, as is all forms of racism and religious intolerance. As long as we are in this world, Christians should work to elevate the dignity and value of every human being, regardless of race or creed, just like Jesus did. The problem with Christian Zionism, however, is that it distorts the plain teachings of the New Testament, taking verses out of context, and then presents itself to the Jewish people as the new face of Christianity.

How have Christian Zionists distorted the New Testament? I can think of a few ways but the most obvious way is either by over-looking or disregarding the fact that Jesus *refused* to support a nationalist agenda for the Jewish people in His day. That's part of the reason why the Jewish leaders hated Him and wanted Him crucified. I find it horrifying that even Christian pastors have told me they believe God's command to Joshua to expel the Canaanites (aka... Palestinians in their mind) still applies today. My question to these pastors is *would Jesus agree?* Think about it. How did Jesus treat the Canaanites of His day? When a Canaanite woman asked Jesus to heal her demonized daughter how did He respond? Did He say sorry lady but you're not supposed to be here? No, He did not. He met her need with compassion and then praised her faith (Matthew 15:21–28). Did Jesus ever give *any* indication that He was interested in picking up where Joshua left off? Since the answer is so painfully obvious, my next question is if Jesus didn't support a nationalist agenda in His day, what makes us think He would support the same thing in our day?

Among the many New Testament passages that Christian Zionists distort, Matthew 25:31–46 is perhaps the most embarrassing. In this passage, Jesus is describing the final judgment where He will tell the righteous, "inasmuch as you've done it to one of the least of these my brethren, you did it to me" and conversely tell the unrighteous, "inasmuch as you did not do it to one of the least of these, you did not do it to Me." Whereas throughout Church history, nearly every Christian has understood this passage to be about feeding the poor, clothing the naked, and visiting the stranger, the Christian Zionist interpretation is that God is going to judge Christians based on whether or not they supported national Israel. The key phrase in this passage for Christian Zionists is *my Brethren*, which, supposedly stands for the Jewish people (and modern day Israel). The problem with this interpretation is that it fails to recognize the simple fact that Jesus defined His "mother" His "sister" and His "brothers" not by natural lineage, but by those who do the will of God (Mark 3:31–35). To define the term "brethren" as the modern nation/state of Israel is a colossal leap of logic.

Another key passage for Christian Zionists is Romans chapter 11. In Romans chapter 11, Paul makes the argument that God hasn't abandoned the Jewish people and makes a stunning prophecy that at some point in the future, there will be a great awakening among the Jewish people in recognizing Jesus as the Messiah. For whatever reason, Christian Zionists take this passage to mean that a future conversion of the Jewish people to Christianity is predicated upon Jews returning to the Biblical Promised Land. This is why Christian Zionist organizations raise millions of dollars every year to immigrate Jews to Israel, even financing Jewish settlers in the West Bank. The problem with this view is that not once in this chapter does Paul mention the words "land" or "nation." Paul was talking about the *spiritual* destiny of the Jewish people, not the *national* destiny.

As much as I can understand why Christian Zionists would want to attach significance to the geographic boundaries of modern day Israel and the earthly city of Jerusalem, it's important to understand that the Bible is progressive revelation, but it only progresses one way and that's in the direction of Jesus Christ. While it may be tempting to isolate certain passages from the Old Testament regarding the land and the city and apply them to the modern world, neither Jesus nor the Apostles interpreted these prophecies in the way they're being applied today.

First, let's talk about the land. Yes, it's true there are certain passages in the Old Testament that indicate God promised the land of Canaan to the physical descendants of Abraham, Isaac, and Jacob to be an "everlasting" possession (Genesis 17:8), but it's also true that the Old Testament describes circumcision as an "everlasting" covenant (Genesis 17:13), and yet the New Testament makes it explicitly clear that the circumcision require-ment has been fulfilled in Jesus and is no longer obligatory. Consider also that on more than one occasion, the Old Testament says that the Aaronic priesthood is an "everlasting" priesthood (see I Chronicles 15:2, 23:13) and yet no credible New Testament scholar disputes the fact that Jesus has superceded the Aaronic priesthood. I find it odd that Isaiah 32:14 teaches that Jerusalem "will become a wasteland forever" and yet I've never found a Christian Zionist who takes *that* verse literally. The point is we shouldn't stretch Biblical words beyond their intended meaning. We must interpret Scripture with Scripture, especially when it comes to older revelation in light of newer revelation.

What does the New Testament teach about the physical possession of the ancient land of Canaan? Not much actually. It doesn't appear to be an issue much on the radar with the Apostles. The writer of Hebrews viewed the possession of the Promised Land as a metaphor for the rest that comes to the Christian that ceases trying to please God on the basis of works (Hebrews 4:8–10). The Apostle Paul broadened the promise God made to Abraham to include not only the Land of Canaan, but also the entire world (Romans 4:13). The Apostle James hearkened back to a famous prophecy in the Book of Amos concerning the restoration of the land to Israel and applied it to the inclusion of Gentiles in God's covenant community (see Amos 9:1–15 and Acts 15:13–17). Perhaps the most famous passage in the Old Testament regarding the restoration of the land to Israel is Ezekiel chapter 37:15–28. It's interesting to note that the second to last verse in this passage, which summarizes the entire chapter, Paul applied directly to the Church (see 2 Corinthians 6:16).

Now let's talk about Jerusalem. If you *really* want to see someone's temperature rise before your eyes, start asking questions about the status of Jerusalem in Middle East peace negotiations and see what kind of reaction you get. For Christians Zionists, the issue is non-negotiable. God wants Jerusalem to be the *exclusive* possession of the Jewish people, and anyone who dares to question this conclusion doesn't believe the Bible is the Word of God. But are Christian Zionists like John Hagee right when they say the Bible would be proven false if Jerusalem didn't remain the exclusive possession of the Jewish people? The answer is *nonsense!* Jerusalem could be overrun by Eskimos and that wouldn't change the truthfulness of Scripture one iota.

What does the New Testament teach about the status of earthly Jerusalem? This is where Christian Zionist arguments *really* fall apart. First, let's look at what the Apostle Paul has to say. In Galatians 4:24–26, the Apostle Paul says:

"For these are the two covenants; the one from Mount Sinai which gives birth to bondage, which is Hagar-for this Hagar is Mount Sinai in Arabia, and corresponds to Jerusalem which now is, and is in bondage with her children, but the Jerusalem above is free, which is the mother of us all."

Notice that Paul compares earthly Jerusalem with Hagar. This is very revealing considering how often Christian Zionists use the fact that Arabs are descendants of Hagar to disqualify them from equal citizenship in Jerusalem. Notice as well what Paul says about the status of earthly Jerusalem. Paul teaches that earthly Jerusalem is "in bondage with her children." Who are the children in bondage that Paul is referring to? The answer is Jews living under the Old Covenant. Hagar corresponds to *Mount Sinai,* the place where Moses gave the Law. Add it all together and you have a startling statement from a first century Jew declaring that those who attribute spiritual significance to earthly Jerusalem, whether Jews under the Old Covenant (or for that matter, Christian Zionists who essentially do the same thing) are the true children of Hagar. Why is this so? Because the *true* Jerusalem is heavenly, not earthly (vs. 26).

The Christian Zionists' political zeal for earthly Jerusalem isn't just a minor theological blunder. It's actually a serious departure from Apostolic teaching. Think about the context of the Book of Hebrews. The Book of Hebrews was written to a group of first century Jews who embraced Jesus as Messiah but were considering a return to Judaism as they had previously understood it, a Judaism focused on land, buildings, temple sacrifices—and the earthly city of Jerusalem. Here is what the writer of Hebrews wrote to the Jewish believers of His day regarding the status of earthly Jerusalem:

"For here we have no continuing city, but we seek the one to come" (Hebrews 13:14).

The writer of Hebrews consistently shifted the focus away from earthly Jerusalem and put the emphasis on the heavenly Jerusalem to come (see also Hebrews 11:15–16, 12:22). This is particularly relevant for our times because if a Christian Zionist had written the Book of Hebrews, the author would have told the first century group of Messianic Jews to "Fight for Jerusalem!" Is it possible to get any further away from apostolic doctrine? Not only do Christian Zionists contradict the writer of Hebrews by telling Jewish believers that they *have* a continuing city on the earth; they want them to be willing to *kill* to make sure the city stays in the hands of Jews!

The odd thing about all this is, even the Old Testament doesn't support what is happening today under the pretext of reclaiming the Biblical Promised land for God (aka… the dream of "Greater Israel"). To prove my point, what's the one chapter in the Old Testament that both Jewish and Christian Zionists refer to that describes God's vision of a newly restored Israel in the clearest and most vivid detail? The answer is Ezekiel 47. This chapter is so specific that it even describes the newly defined borders of a restored Israel. Given that this chapter is the clearest depiction of God's idea of a restored Promised Land, I find it a bit suspicious that I've never heard a Christian Zionist leader teach on the last two verses, which say:

"It shall be that you will divide it by lot as an inheritance for yourselves, and for the strangers who dwell among you and who bear children among you. *They shall be to you as native born among the children of Israel;* they shall have an inheritance with you among the tribes of Israel. And it shall be that in *whatever tribe the stranger dwells, there you shall give him his inheritance,'* says the Lord God." (italics emphasis mine)

Clearly what Ezekiel had in mind was equal rights for Jews and strangers alike in the restored Promised Land. Ezekiel's vision sounds much more like the yearning of a Martin Luther King than the battle cry of a Pat Robertson or a Hal Lindsey—and Ezekiel's vision is far from an isolated passage. Even if we grant that the land belongs to Jews, that doesn't negate the *overwhelming* emphasis of the Biblical prophets that God's people are not to oppress the aliens and the strangers living in the land. It would require a lobotomy to read the Biblical prophets and claim they would have supported land confiscations and home demolitions for the purpose of building settlements for Jews *only*—and then building roads that connect them that aliens and strangers (aka Palestinians) are unable to access.

The problem with Christian Zionism is that it reverses the order of God's progressive revelation, and because of this reversal, their positions and their actions are filled with contradictions. Christian Zionists spend millions of dollars every year to fund Jewish immigration to Israel even though they believe two thirds of them are going to be wiped out by a nuclear holocaust in the not-too-distant future—in Israel. Contrast this with Jesus who advised the Jewish people of His day to *get out* of Jerusalem before the inevitable bloodbath of 70 A.D (Luke 21:20–21). Christian Zionists want to drag the world into war to rebuild the Jewish Temple, even though they believe the temple will then go on to be desecrated by the *anti-Christ*. Can someone please explain to me why I as a Christian am obligated to support an agenda of racial superiority for Jews in national Israel when according to the same belief system, the same national Israel is going to be led by the *anti-Christ* in the not too distant future?

I realize that there are those who will read everything that I've written in this chapter so far and still feel that it's their Biblical obligation to support national Israel and work against a two state solution—or any solution for that matter—to the Israeli/Palestinian conflict. I further realize that the Bible is a difficult book to interpret, especially when it comes to figuring out how the Old Covenant and the New Covenant relate to each other. I take Hebrews 8:13 at face value when it says the Old Covenant is "obsolete", so that rules out every argument based from Mount Sinai on that says Israel is supposed to wipe out the Canaanites (Never mind the fact that Christians who use this argument balk at the term ethnic cleansing to describe what's going on today while appealing to Old Testament texts that advocate *genocide* to justify their position). I know there are some who will say that the Land Covenant *precedes* the law and is therefore based on God's unconditional promise to Abraham.

Very well then. I'll temporarily concede this point—debatable as it may be. What I intend to show now is *even if we appeal to God's original promise to Abraham,* that still doesn't preclude an agreement for exchanging land for the sake of peace. One can argue against this based on politics or pragmatism, but not based on the Bible. If we look at the lives of Abraham and Isaac, we see that both men were committed to claiming the land *peacefully.* Neither Abraham nor Isaac conquered the land through force. As a matter of fact, both men entered into negotiations with the original inhabitants of the land. In Genesis chapter 26:13–31, we see that Isaac moved *three different times* when the

Philistines stopped up his wells. If we were to judge Isaac by Christian Zionist standards, we'd have to call Isaac's actions "appeasement," but notice what verse 31 says:

"Then they arose early in the morning and swore an oath with one another: and Isaac sent them away, and they departed from him in peace."

I wonder why Christian Zionists feel they have to be stricter in their interpretation of dividing the land than *the very men to whom the promises were made?*

Lastly, Jesus gave one—and only one—criteria for which the world can distinguish true disciples from false disciples, and that's love for the brethren (John 13:35). Both James and John elaborate on this by stating that love for the brethren must always go beyond mere sentiment and translate itself into concrete action (James 2:15–17, I John 3:16–18). Every single time the word brethren is mentioned in the New Testament, it refers exclusively to believers in Jesus. It never refers to non-believers—even non-believing Jews. With that in mind, how is it even possible that so many "evangelical" Christians side with unbelieving Jews over and against their Palestinian Christian brethren?

How long is it going to take till American Christians realize that it's not only *Muslims* that are affected by home demolitions and land confiscations, but *our brothers and sisters in Christ* are also affected? I hereby give an open challenge to *anyone* who would challenge me on this to go to Bethlehem, meet with Palestinian Christians personally (Bethlehem Bible College would be a good place to start), listen to their stories, and if you're *still* not convinced that supporting the expansion of Jewish settlements is a direct violation of the command of Jesus to love the brethren, then all I can say is, "Choose ye this day whom you will serve."

When the dust settles and the smoke clears, what you have in the Middle East is two "peoples" living in the same land. One group claims the land is theirs by divine right. The other group claims the land is theirs by historical right, and the thing that bugs me the most is I'm still not sure if I'm objective. Now that I've seen what the other sides of the story looks like, I'm not even sure if objectivity is possible anymore. Whether we look at a situation from an insiders' perspective or from an outsiders' perspective, all of us interact with the world around us based on presuppositions that determine how we interpret everything we see, hear, taste, touch, and smell. Sometimes our presuppositions are right. Other times they're dead wrong.

Though many things remain unclear to me regarding the Israeli/Palestinian conflict, what's crystal clear to me is this conflict is clearly a conflict between the powerful and the powerless, the Israelis being the powerful and the Palestinians being the powerless. What is also clear to me is this isn't merely a conflict of Jews versus Arabs or Israelis versus Palestinians. Rather, it's a conflict between Israeli and Palestinian war-makers versus Israeli and Palestinian peacemakers. Both sides have villains who want to drive the other into the sea and heroes who work tirelessly for peace and reconciliation. Also on both sides are the vast majority of people who are neither heroes nor villains, but ordinary people who want peace on one hand, but fear for their safety and well being on the other hand.

On our last day in Hebron, I was pleased to be able to take part in a symbolic action helping a Palestinian farmer and his family harvests their olive trees. On the man's property, Jewish settlers have built a sidewalk cutting through the man's orchard and nearly every day they walk through his property with guns in their pockets, hate in their eyes, and threats on their lips. What gave me hope that day was seeing an Israeli peace activist that I had met earlier on the trip working side by side with the Palestinian farmer helping him pick olives from his olive tree. On that day a thought entered my mind that's been with me ever since and refuses to let me go to sleep at night.

Which is more Christ-like? The TV evangelist who cheered in 2006 as Israeli warplanes were dropping bombs on buses and bridges in Lebanon, calling the action a "miracle from God"—or the liberal Jew picking olives with a Palestinian farmer? Even more nagging is this question. What does it say about the state of the Church in America when an American Christian has to write an entire book to defend his orthodox credentials for picking option number two?

CHAPTER 10

Removing the Plank

A fter I returned home from my encounter with Khalid, I poured myself into the task of reading books, scrutinizing the TV news, and watching just about every documentary I could get my hands on—anything to help me understand the broader socio-political context in which our nation finds itself today. One of the films that I watched was Errol Morris's 2004 Oscar-winning documentary *The Fog of War*, a film that never achieved blockbuster status, but is arguably one of the most important historical documentaries ever made. What gives *The Fog of War* its significance is the way it allows the viewer to see some of the most crucial moments in 21st century American history through the eyes of former Secretary of Defense Robert McNamara—a man who held one of the highest positions of power in our nation.

Throughout the film, McNamara recalls his bird's eye view of the Cuban Missile Crisis and the Vietnam War as a member of both

Johnson and Kennedy's inner circle. Though much of the film puts McNamara on display lecturing viewers on the finer aspects of foreign policy, the chilling aspect of the film lies in McNamara's demeanor. McNamara appears to be troubled by the ramifications of the decisions he made throughout his career in the Oval office, though he mysteriously stops short of an apology. The viewer gets the impression that, in McNamara's world, his final lecture to humanity is his atonement. For those that lived through the Cuban Missile Crisis and the tumultuous years of the Vietnam War, it's McNamara's first lesson that turns out to be the gut grabber—empathize with your enemy.

At a time when the U.S.A. and the U.S.S.R. were threatening each other with nuclear annihilation, few and far between were the voices that called for moderation. One of those voices was Ambassador Thompson, a man who—literally—saved the world. During the Cuban Missile Crisis, Kennedy's Joint Chiefs of Staff worked overtime to convince the President to launch a preemptive military strike against Cuba to take out the tactical nuclear weapons pointed at American soil. Thompson, who was serving as the U.S. ambassador to Cuba at the time, was one of the few voices that urged restraint. Thompson argued that Kruschev, the Soviet ambassador to the U.S. at the time, would want to tell his people back home that he had saved Cuba from imminent invasion. It was based on this understanding that Thompson felt Kruschev would be willing to negotiate. Though it was a difficult call, Kennedy took Thompson's advice over the advice of his military advisors—and the world was spared an unspeakable disaster.

The heart-wrenching part is watching McNamara praise Thompson's wisdom as a man that spared the world an unnecessary catastrophe because he took the time to understand his enemy—and then watching McNamara contrast Thompson's wisdom with his own role (howbeit an ambivalent one) in the escalation of the Vietnam conflict. McNamara pulls no punches in letting the audience know that the prevailing wisdom at the time—namely that Vietnam was a pawn of China and that if the country fell to Communism it would have a domino effect on the rest of the world—was wrong. In a manner eerily similar to that of a confession booth, McNamara reminds the audience that the U.S. dropped two to three times as many bombs on Southeast Asia as all of the bombs dropped on Western Europe in World War II.

Here's McNamara in his own words:

"What makes us omniscient? Have we a record of omniscience? We are the strongest nation in the world today. I do not believe we should ever apply that economic, political, or military power unilaterally. If we had followed that rule in Vietnam, *we wouldn't have been there!* (italics emphasis mine). None of our allies supported us; not Japan, not Germany, not Britain or France. If we can not persuade nations with comparable values, of the merit of our cause, we must reexamine our reasoning."

The moment I heard McNamara speak these words, that's when things got personal for me. Being born in 1978, I never served in Vietnam and neither do I know of a close relative that died in the conflict, but when I was a student in Bible School I walked the streets of Saigon in another capacity—as a short term missionary. Both times I was in Vietnam my group visited the War Remnants museum in Saigon, a museum filled with images of atrocities committed by the U.S. military against the Vietnamese people. In one image, there's a soldier holding a gun to a civilian woman's head. In anther image, there's a soldier laughing over the charred remains of a Viet Cong killed by a Napalm bomb. In still other images there's an airplane spraying Agent Orange over civilian villages. The museum also contains photos of emaciated children born with severe deformities as a result of the Agent Orange. Perhaps the most ironic image for me, a "pro-life" Christian that supported the Iraq war, was the image of stillborn babies—babies born dead as a direct result of the U.S. military's use of weapons of mass destruction.

What I find even more disturbing is that, even after seeing images of the charred bodies and the still born babies, it never occurred to me that my country could have been wrong in attacking Vietnam. Not only did I not question the morality of invading a nation that hadn't attacked us, I never even questioned it from a tactical point of view. I never questioned whether the billions of dollars spent on bombing Vietnam could have been put to better use building infrastructure in my own country. To ask that question would have been—ironically—unpatriotic. Every one else was moved to tears except for me, the zealous Christian missionary who traveled land and sea to teach others about the man who taught His followers to love their enemies. How ironic is it that it took a lecture from the *former U.S. Secretary of*

Defense to finally convince a devoted follower of Jesus that the Vietnam invasion was wrong!

The lessons don't stop there. It's one thing to challenge the legitimacy of the Vietnam War. It's quite another to challenge the sacred Holy Grail for those who believe in the possibility of a just war—the morality of the U.S. military during World War II. Surprisingly, McNamara refuses to let us off the hook even when it comes to holy World War II. In perhaps the most disturbing part of the film, McNamara recalls his role as an advisor to General Curtis Le May and how one of his suggestions to the General went far beyond his expectations. We all know about the atomic bombs dropped on Hiroshima and Nagasaki—bombs that killed roughly 220,000 people—but how many of us know about the intensive firebombing campaign waged against 67 *Japanese* cities before the nukes were dropped? Not only did the campaign end up destroying 58% of Yokohama, 99% of Toyama, and 40 % of Nuguya, but; as McNamara painfully recalls, in *one night alone* firebombs killed 100,000 civilians in Tokyo. Is it possible that if it were *our* cities and 100,000 of *our* civilians being firebombed, we might call that terrorism today? Something to think about.

If we're going to talk about proportionality, which is one of the cornerstones of just war theory, the Pearl Harbor invasion aimed at a military target, not civilians. And, by the way, the Japanese used the doctrine of preemption to justify their invasion. The invasion killed 2,403 people, only 68 of them being civilians. [33]

---

[33] http://wiki.answers.com/Q/
How_many_people_died_in_the_attack_on_Pearl_Harbor
Accessed July 18th, 2008

According to McNamara, had the U.S. lost the war, he and many of the top U.S. commanders would have been tried for war crimes. Now that he's nearing the end of his life, McNamara is asking the questions that most of us who prefer to live in a black and white world in which we're the heroes and everyone else are the villains would rather not ask. "What makes it immoral if you lose but not if you win?" asks McNamara.

McNamara has a point. A common tendency among human beings is to separate the world into "us" versus "them", empathizing with those whom we perceive to be "us" and dehumanizing everyone that we perceive to be "them." The interests of those whom we perceive to be "us" need to be protected no matter what the moral cost is to those we perceive to be "them". The "thems" are at best an inconvenience or at worst our enemies. Even the "thems" that have little to do with the conflict between "us" and "them"—like innocent civilians—are disposable commodities to serve the interests of "us." The tragedy in all of this is the Body of Christ is supposed to be a spiritual entity that transcends artificial "us" versus "them" distinctions, especially the ones created by national boundaries.

I can remember when I was in the 8th grade attending a Christian school during the first Persian Gulf War. Every day my classmates and I would report to each other the latest we had heard about the U.S. military's progress in ousting Saddam Hussein from Kuwait. Our youth pastor at the time made it abundantly clear that the war had nothing to do with oil and that it was our duty to pray for the success of our soldiers. When the war was over, all of us were ecstatic at how quickly the victory came and how few casualties there were. Our nation's military lost a record low of 400 men in one of the most decisive victories in military history.

Here's the part that bothers me today. Nobody thought it significant to tell us that the casualties on the other side were between 20,000 and 100,000. [34] Neither did anyone see it necessary to tell us about the devastating bombing campaign against Iraq's civilian infrastructure. The U.S. bombing campaign destroyed nearly every dam, pumping station, water sewage treatment plants, railroad, bridge, and electric power station in the country. [35] Before the war, Iraq was on the verge of becoming a first world nation and we literally bombed them back to the Stone Age. But none of that mattered at the time. All that mattered was how few casualties were suffered on "our" side and the fact that "we" won. Little did we know at the time that the U.S. intervention in Gulf One, followed by a 10-year bombing campaign and sanctions responsible for the death of 500,000 Iraqi children, would become one of the primary recruiting tools for Bin Laden in the formation of Al-Qaida prior to 9/11. So can we really say that we "won" Gulf one? What would have happened had the United States *not* intervened and massacred so many Muslims? We'll never know.

I believe that the chief problem in the Church today, especially the American Church, is that, by and large, we've bought into the idea that believing in Jesus has little to do following His

---

34 http://en.wikipedia.org/wiki/Gulf_War
Accessed July 18th, 2008
35 ibid

teachings. It's as if by some mass hypnosis, the collective Church has heard the voice of Jesus saying, "Forget about my life and teachings. The real reason why I came to earth was to bear the penalty for your sins, not to teach you how to live." The odd part about this is the problem doesn't stem from a lack of sincerity. Every Christian that I know at least wants to think they're following Jesus the best that they can. The problem is that very few Christians that I know think the teachings of Jesus are relevant for today. We treat Jesus as if He were an impractical idealist, a bit too spacey to give us any guidance for the real world. We sing His praises on Sunday morning, but when it comes to entrusting our lives to His moral brilliance, Jesus has lots of fans, but very few followers.

Nowhere is this more evident than the way the average American Christian thinks about how Jesus' admonition to "Remove the plank from your own eye" might relate to violence against others. One of the most common responses I get when I share the idea that following Jesus entails a commitment to non-violence is "That's great Aaron, but you should be teaching that to Muslims, not to us." The assumption is that it's only wrong when the other side engages in violence against us, not when we engage in violence against them.

Let me say first that I understand exactly where those who take this line of reasoning are coming from. When I hear of Muslims marching into churches in countries like Sudan, Pakistan, Indonesia, and Eritrea and indiscriminately slaughtering Christians, it makes me sick to my stomach. I'm also well aware of the persecution that many Muslims around the world face when they convert to Christianity. Often they're tortured, killed, imprisoned either by their governments or—worse—by their own families.

The problem with taking these extreme examples and using them to characterize the entire population of the world's 1.3 billion Muslims is, according to the best data that we have available, the vast majority of Muslims in the world also condemn this type of extremism. [36] It does little good to characterize an entire group of people by the extremist fringe, even if the fringe is a sizable fringe. In the decades up to and during the civil rights era, the fiercest opponents of racial equality weren't godless liberals, but conservative fundamentalist Christians—people that constituted a majority at the time—and yet how many of us today would agree with the statement that Christians are racist? The claim would have certainly seemed credible 60 years ago in Birmingham, Alabama, and it would have been wrong.

It's a universal truth that, "in whatever you judge another you condemn yourself; for you who judge practice the same things" (Romans 2:1). Not only does this apply on the individual level, but also on a civilization level. It wasn't too long ago in the scheme of history that Christians in the West were also slaying and torturing infidels in the name of Christ. The crusades, the inquisition, and the religious wars of the 1600's are but a few examples. The

---

36 The most comprehensive research ever done on the thoughts of the worlds 1.3 billion Muslims is revealed in the book *Who Speaks for Islam? What a Billion Muslims Really Think* (Gallup Press, 2007)

genocide of entire native populations in the Western Hemisphere is another example, though that was largely motivated by greed, not piety. Even worse, the carnage of World War I and World War II, including Hitler's Nazi Germany, took place in the most Christianized region in the world at the time. Even if we look at the violence between Sunnis and Shiites in Post-Saddam Iraq, the level of barbarism is at least on the same level (if not below) as the Christian on Christian violence that took place in Rwanda in 1994 where ethnic Hutus slaughtered roughly 1 million Tutsis—with the help of their priests and pastors. Before we go making blanket condemnations against the Muslim world, it might be a good idea to ask ourselves how is it possible that the Christian world could have ever tolerated such violence in our own backyards.

In the months leading up to my debate with Khalid, I had already gone through a grueling round of interviews from Stephen Marshall, the director of "Holy Wars." Knowing that I was representing Christian missionaries everywhere, I did my best to answer Marshall's questions the best that I knew how. For most of the questions, I knew the standard apologetic answers, but there was one question that continued to nag at me even while I was sitting in the hot seat across from Khalid. Khalid wouldn't have understood the question, so I dared not bring it up then, but here's the question that kept rolling around in my head, and it's one of the primary objections to the gospel raised by postmodern thinkers:

Religions create cultures, cultures reinforce tribal and national identities, tribal and national identities lead to competition for resources and prejudice against other human beings, and competition and prejudice lead to violent conflict. In short, religion leads to war.

As tempting as it may be to dismiss this line of reasoning, I think the challenge deserves careful consideration. The first line of defense that many apologists have taken is to say that even without religion people would still find ways to divide themselves either by tribal/national identity or by political and economic philosophies. True, but unfortunately this answer doesn't quite cut it. The thing that religion provides is a *transcendent source* that allows people to reinforce their sense of superiority over others. It's one thing to say "You're inferior to me because of the color of your skin." It's another thing to say, "You're inferior to me because *God* says you're inferior." Religion provides a means by which human beings can dehumanize others *with the approval of their conscience.*

The funny thing is, it doesn't seem to matter which religion we're talking about. Conventional wisdom in liberal academia says that the monotheistic religions like Christianity and Islam are more prone to violence because of the exclusivity of their claims, but that's pure fantasy. Hindus and Buddhists are every bit as militant in persecuting people of other faiths, just ask Christians living in countries like India, Laos, and Myanmar. It doesn't matter whether we're talking about Christian versus Muslims or Muslims versus Christians. History has sufficiently proven that when religion—and yes—even Christianity— becomes fused with tribal/national identity, the results are deadly. Whether we're talking about the Armenian genocide at the turn of last century or the ethnic cleansing of Bosnian Muslims that took place in the decade of the 90's, the evidence is compelling. Religion and nationalism don't mix.

For the record, none of this undermines my faith in the Lord Jesus Chris as the unique Savior of the World. On the contrary, my faith in Jesus is strengthened like never before. It's precisely *because* of religion's tendency to legitimize violence and reinforce tribal identity that *all* religious adherents—no matter what religion they follow—need to cling to an absolute standard of non-violence, and it's on this point that Jesus shines the most. The chief moral contribution that Jesus gave to the world is the gospel of the kingdom, and it's precisely the gospel of the kingdom that seeks to create a people on the earth that categorically reject violence and nationalism—even as instruments for achieving moral ends.

In all this I'm not saying that we have to embrace the idea that some in far-left circles have taken, namely that *we're* the bad guys and *they're* the good guys. That's ridiculous! Political reality is never *that* black and white. There are always shades of grey when it comes to violent conflict between two competing socio-political groups. All I'm saying is in order to win the War on Terror it might be a good idea to know the enemy and understand what's fueling their hatred against us. In meeting Khalid, I came up against a set of religious values and political beliefs that are shared by fundamentalist Muslims from Morocco to Indonesia, beliefs which are polar to those widely held in the West. And these conflicting ideas are driving the world into a conflict that could one day become civilizational, West versus East, Islam vs. the predominantly Christian democracies.

I can remember living in Senegal and talking with people wearing Osama Bin Laden T-shirts and they were no more of a terrorist than you or I. Their attitude was, "Osama bin Laden is my hero. Now, let's have some tea." This is why my conversation with Khalid shook me so deeply to the core. I knew that it wasn't just *extremists* that shared his grievances against the West, but normal every day Muslims who go to work, love their families, and watch the evening news, just like the vast majority of people I know in America. I suddenly realized that even if we used our military resources to capture and kill terrorists around the world; that alone isn't going to solve the problem. For every terrorist we capture or kill, there will be two or three more to replace them, and we can't simply blow away 1.2 billion Muslims from the face of the earth.

We tend not to listen to people who support terrorists, but I think that may be our most profound weakness. Because if you actually sit down and listen to them, like I chose to do with Khalid, you will hear an anger and frustration with America and the Western world that isn't emerging from a vacuum. One of the things I learned was that we Americans have a totally different idea of when this conflict actually started. We see 9/11 as the beginning of the War on Terror, but many, if not most Muslims around the world see it very differently. In much of the Islamic world, 9/11 was a long-coming retaliation, reaction to abuses from the West that date back to the formation of Israel, and more recently, the first Gulf War and subsequent sanctions and bombing that not only destroyed much of the civilian infrastructure in Iraq, but also killed hundreds of thousands of Muslims. To the average Muslim on the street from Morocco all the way to Indonesia, it doesn't matter that the people that were killed were *Iraqis*, what matters is that they were *Muslims*.

It's crucial to understand that most people in the Muslim world don't group themselves in the same way that we do in the West. For example, if a country were to attack Columbia or Venezuela, very few of us would think of it as a jihad against Christianity. That's because we tend to group ourselves by our national identity first, and religious identity second. We think of ourselves as Americans and people living in Columbia as Columbians. Most Muslims, on the other hand, view themselves as Muslims first and citizens of their nation-state second. This is why *any* military intervention in the Muslim world from the outside will always be viewed as a war against Islam, as was the case in Gulf One when the U.S. intervened to oust Saddam Hussein from Kuwait. Let's not forget that it was U.S. imposed sanctions that killed 500,000 children in Iraq, the presence of US troops in Muslim lands, and U.S. support of corrupt and oppressive leaders in countries like Egypt, Pakistan, and Saudi Arabia, these three complaints were the primary recruiting points Bin Laden, and many others like him, used to attract people to radical Islam.

Lest you think that all this talk about dialogue and understanding is reserved for bleeding heart hippies, the fiercest critic of the neoconservative strategy of permanent war and occupation of Muslim lands is none other than Michael Schaeuer—the former head of the CIA's Bin Laden unit. While Schaeuer is by no means a pacifist, the message in his book *Imperial Hubris* can be summarized by saying that we may think that Bin Laden and his followers attacked our nation because they hate our freedom, but we delude ourselves at our own peril. The real reason why they attacked us is because of our foreign policy. Yes, it's true that they despise Western decadence, but that's not what's motivating them to come over and kill us. They hate us because we're over there. Schaeuer's book confirms that had our nation's leaders taken time to understand what's motivating radical Muslims to attack U.S. soil, we would have known that invading Iraq would actually *increase* the support for Al-Qaida and like-minded terrorist groups targeting U.S. interests—which it in fact did.

Another man that's arrived at the same conclusion is Robert Pape, author of *Dying to Win: the Logic of Suicide Terrorism*. When Pape researched every suicide attack in the world from 1980–2004, he came to a startling conclusion. In Pape's own words:

"The central fact is that overwhelmingly suicide terrorist attacks are not driven by religion as much as they are by a clear strategic objective: to compel modern democracies to withdraw military forces from the territory that the terrorists view as their home- land. From Lebanon to Sri Lanka to Chechnya to Kashmir to the

West Bank, every major suicide terrorist campaign—more than 95% of all the incidents—has had as its central objective to compel a democratic state to withdraw." [37]

If our nation were serious about eroding the support base for radical Islam, then we'd devote our resources to education and social development in the Muslim world, not to an over-inflated military budget that polices the world and occupies other countries. Tragically, much of the aid money the Bush administration promised for reconstruction in Afghanistan was diverted to the invasion of Iraq. It's this lack of long- term thinking that seriously tarnishes America's image around the world and reinforces what most of the world's 1.3 billion Muslims already think—that the U.S. is only interested in promoting democracy to the extent that it serves U.S. oil interests. What our nation lacks at this crucial juncture in our history is creative thinking, and the reason why we lack creative thinking is because of our unwavering faith in the myth of redemptive violence, especially in the Church. At the time of this writing, Saudi Arabian oil sheiks are spending billions of dollars building madrassas (extremist schools of the Wahabbi sect) in Afghanistan and Pakistan and, yet, how many of us think of energy independence as a national security issue?

In his book *Three Cups of Tea*, author David Oliver Renin tells the story of a man named Greg Mortenson who's spent the last ten years building secular schools in the heart of Waziristan, the most remote and extreme corner of Pakistan. After the U.S. government heard about Mortenson's work, the Pentagon invited him to

---

37 This quote is taken from *Who Speaks for Islam?*, 77

meet with some of the top military leaders of our nation, including Donald Rumsfeld. Here's what Mortenson had to say to them:

"'I'm not a military expert,' Mortenson said. 'And these figures might not be exactly right. But as best as I can tell, we've launched 114 Tomahawk cruise missiles into Afghanistan so far. Now take the cost of one of those missiles tipped with a Raytheon guidance system, which I think is about $840,000. For that much money, you could build dozens of schools that could provide tens of thousands of students with a balanced nonextremist education over the course of a generation. Which do you think will make us more secure?" [38]

Lastly, the most comprehensive research ever done on the opinions of the world's 1.3 billion Muslims was undertaken by Gallup research. Between 2001 and 2007, Gallup research conducted tens of thousands of hour-long, face-to-face interviews with residents of more than 35 nations that are predominately Muslims or have substantial Muslim populations. In a long awaited book *Who Speaks for Islam*, Gallup researchers reveal the answers to the questions that have been nagging Americans ever since September 11th, 2001. What they found was that roughly 7% of the Islamic world can be classified as politically radicalized, the definition of politically radicalized being determined by a positive response to the question of whether 9/11 was completely justified.

Out of this 7%, very few cited the Koran to justify their position on 9/11 and, perhaps more significantly, the vast majority of them

---

38 *Three Cups of Tea* (Penguin Books, 2007), 294–295

said that the best way for America to improve relations with the Muslim world is *not* to change who and what we are, but to respect their religion and to change the policies they deem to be prejudiced and unfair against Muslims. Furthermore, they discovered that the primary motivation behind Islamic radicalism is the threat of Western (and in particular the U.S.) domination and occupation of Muslim lands.

Lest I be misunderstood, I'm *not* saying that the U.S. should appease terrorism by sitting down and having a cup of tea with Bin-Laden. Neither am I saying that the U.S. government shouldn't pursue an aggressive strategy in cooperation with our allies and international law enforcement to pursue Al-Qaida, freeze their assets, arrest the murderers and bring them to justice. What I *am* saying is permanent war and occupation is a strategy that not only doesn't work, it blurs the distinction between good and evil and causes us to become the very thing we oppose.

Perhaps the most shocking statistic of Gallup's research is that *Muslims* on average are more likely than Americans to unequivocally condemn attacks on civilians. According to Gallup's research, only 46% of Americans think that bombing and other attacks aimed at civilians are never justified. Compare this number with 86% in Pakistan and 80% in—ironically—Iran. Conversely, only 2% in Iran and 4% in Saudi Arabia believe attacks aimed directly at civilians are completely justified while the number in the U.S. is 6%. [39] Perhaps Jesus knew what He was

---

39 ibid

talking about after all when He said, "First remove the plank in your own eye before removing the speck in your brother's eye." Heart rending, gut grabbing, no-holds-barred plank removing may not save the world, but it very well could save our souls.

CHAPTER 11

Powerless Prophets

F ew books in the Bible contain the shock and the horror as the history recorded in the Book of Judges. There's a reason why the Sunday- School version emphasizes Gideon's valiant 300 and Samson's bad hair day. Imagine a Precious Moments version of Jael driving a tent peg into Sisera's temple, Ehud driving a dagger into King Eglon's giant belly, or an elderly Levite calling a nation to war by cutting his concubine into 12 pieces! The Book of Judges has it all for an NC17 rating. Blood. Lust. Power. Passion. We can look away from it if we must, but then we'd have to look away from the rest of human history.

As comforting as it might be to think humanity has progressed since ancient times, all we have to do is look at the death and destruction of the 20th century to know that modernization isn't the savior we thought it would be. Now instead of manly swords and spears we have weapons of mass destruction. Even an overweight intellectual in a business suit could potentially push a button and wipe out tens of thousands of people—all while chowing down on a Big Mac. Institutionalized power may not be the testosterone driven force it used to be, with men swinging battle axes while showing off their burly biceps, but its effects have the potential for greater destruction and misery than ever before.

Go to any museum in any part of the world and the bulk of what you'll see is kings and chiefs marching off to war against other kings and chiefs for the purpose of conquering land and controlling resources—all with the blessing of a tribal deity. The cycle of power has been going on for so long that few have been able to free their minds to imagine a world without kings, presidents, prime ministers, borders, armies, police, and CEO's. Those who have are usually called anarchists.

While the term anarchist covers a broad range of groups and ideologies, the core idea of anarchist philosophy is that power is not self-justifying. When human beings exercise power over other human beings, the burden of proof is always on the one exercising the power to justify why he or she should be given the power. One of the most famous anarchist philosophers of our time is MIT linguistics professor Noam Chomsky. In his book *Interventions*, Chomsky writes:

"The great soul of power extends far beyond states, to every domain of life, from families to international affairs. And throughout, every form of authority and domination bears a severe burden of proof. It is not self-legitimizing. And when it cannot bear the burden, as is commonly the case, it should be dismantled." [40]

Notice how Chomsky does *not* say that human governments should be overthrown with violence, and neither does he give a description of an ideal society. Despite the stereotype, anarchist philosophy at its core is neither violent nor utopian. All anarchism says is that power isn't self-legitimizing, therefore illegitimate power structures should be dismantled. It's still up to human beings to figure out which authority structures are legitimate and which authority structures are illegitimate. An example of legitimate authority that Chomsky gives would be a parent using force to stop a child from running in front of a moving train. An obvious example of illegitimate authority is the institution of slavery.

Another figure in U.S. history with an anarchist bent is Henry David Thoreau. While Thoreau is mostly known for his two-year experiment in essential living on the shore of Walden Pond, it was his essay entitled "Civil Disobedience" that eventually inspired luminaries like Gandhi and Martin Luther King to resist unjust authority in their day. Thoreau directly challenged the idea that the state is the guarantor of human liberty. Like Thomas Jefferson, Thoreau saw a standing army as fundamentally opposed to human liberty, but unlike Jefferson, Thoreau further concluded that the standing army is merely an arm of the standing government, and the government that requires the standing army is simply a tool of the people to execute their will against the interests of others. The question Thoreau asked in his day was

---

40 Noam Chomsky, *Interventions* (City Light Books, 2007), 217

why should human beings subordinate their conscience to the State? In Thoreau's own words:

"Can there not be a government in which majorities do not decide right and wrong—but conscience?—in which majorities only decide those questions to which the rule of expediency is applicable? Must the citizen ever for a moment, or in the least degree, resign his conscience to a legislator? Why has every man a conscience, then? I think that we should be men first, and subjects afterward. It is not desirable to cultivate a respect for law, so much as for the right."

Herein lies the conundrum. On the one hand, it seems obvious that human beings need to entrust a degree of power to other human beings to prevent civilization from descending into chaos, but on the other hand the solution often creates more problems than it supposedly solves. Power tends to corrupt and absolute power tends to corrupt absolutely. Even when 51% of the population rule over 49% of the population—which oddly enough we call that freedom—institutionalized power still relies on the use of force to coerce people to do things against their will.

The Book of Judges demonstrates the problem from both sides of the equation. The Book closes with, "In those days there was no king in Israel; everyone did what was right in their own eyes," (Judges 21:25) but then we also have a curious parable that seems to indicate that the exercise of power inhibits man's natural potential. In Judges 9:7–15 we read:

"The trees once went forth to anoint a king over them. And they said to the olive tree, 'Reign over us!' But the olive tree said to them, 'Should I cease giving my oil, with which they honor God and men, and go to sway over trees?' Then the trees said to the fig tree, 'You come and reign over us!' But the fig tree said to them, 'Should I cease my sweetness and my good fruit, and go to sway over trees?' Then the trees said to the vine, 'You come and reign over us!' But the vine said to them, 'Should I cease my new wine, which cheers both God and men, and go to sway over trees?' Then all the trees said to the bramble, 'You come and reign over us!' And the bramble said to the trees, 'If in truth you anoint me as king over you, then come and take shelter in my shade; But if not, let fire come out of the bramble and devour the cedars of Lebanon!'"

If we look at the puzzle from a Biblical perspective, the problem becomes clear. Man is fallen and therefore needs law and order to protect the innocent, but when human beings exercise power over other human beings they tend to use it in sinful ways. Institutionalized power tends to reinforce tribal and religious loyalties thereby creating worldly kingdoms, and worldly kingdoms tend to advance their interests against other worldly kingdoms by the power of the sword. Institutionalized power also tends to create ruling classes, and ruling classes tend to create economic inequality. When the poor finally get around to overthrowing their overlords, they create new ruling classes and the cycle starts all over again. All of these evils stem from the abuse of power—the very power that seems so absolutely necessary to keep the human race from spinning out of control. The question then becomes what is God's solution to this tangled web we've weaved for ourselves? Do we create a theocracy or do we abolish the State?

According to the Apostle Paul, God's answer to the problem of institutionalized power creating worldly kingdoms is *not* to try to overthrow worldly kingdoms or even to try to reform worldly kingdoms; God's answer is to create an entirely new entity altogether—an entity called the Church that instead of ruling *over* people by the power of force, rules *under* people but by the power of suffering redemptive love. This is what God was aiming for all along even throughout the narrative of the Old Testament. As Paul writes in Ephesians 3:8–11:

"To me, who am less than the least of all the saints, this grace was given, that I should preach among the Gentiles the unsearchable riches of Christ, and to make all see what is the fellowship of the mystery, which from the beginning of the ages has been hidden in God who created all things through Jesus Christ; *to the intent that now* the manifold wisdom of God might be made known by the Church to the principalities and powers in the heavenly places" (italics emphasis mine).

The Church is called to manifest the reign of God by imitating Calvary, and by imitating Calvary the Church exposes the inadequacy of power systems built on violence—like modern nation states. Thoreau wasn't a fan of the Bible, but had Thoreau been able to ask the Apostle Paul the question of whether it's better for a man or woman to live by law or by conscience, he probably would have been surprised to hear Paul answer that it's better to live by conscience. To the degree that the Church lives out its calling of men and women living by the higher law of their Christ-indwelt consciences, challenging unjust power structures, the Church becomes an alternative society that serves as a counter-force to earthly kingdoms built on violence.

If we understand the Bible as a narrative, we can see that in the beginning Adam and Eve exercised dominion over *nature*, not over each other (Genesis 1:28). If we view the Garden of Eden as humanity's ideal state, then we have to conclude that dominion and authority isn't God's ideal for how human beings are supposed to relate to each other. The first mention of a domination/subjugation relationship between human beings is when God told Eve that she would desire her husband and that her husband would rule over her. But notice that the domination/subjugation relationship is a direct result of the curse. It's not the ideal state (Genesis 3:16). Everything we read in the Bible from Genesis 4 onward is God working with humanity to bring humanity back to its original state of perfection, where human beings no longer rule over each other but serve each other in love.

We can see this progression even when we read the Old Testament. When Cain killed Abel, God didn't prescribe the death penalty; rather He put a mark on his head to keep others from retaliating (Genesis 4:15). The law of first mentions demands that we take this to mean that God's highest ideal for dealing with violent crime is non-retaliation, much like what we see in Jesus. It wasn't until after the flood—nearly a thousand years later—that we see any semblance of a divinely ordained government, and even here there's no complicated hierarchy, just a simple rule that says, "Whoever shed's man's blood, by man his blood shall be shed" (Genesis 9:6). This may not have been God's ideal, but it was necessary at the time.

The problem is once laws are introduced, institutionalized power to enforce the laws nearly always follows, and institutionalized power turns into earthly kingdoms—and that's precisely what happened. The first mention of the word "kingdom" in Scripture is Genesis 10:10 and that kingdom was the kingdom of Babel founded by Nimrod. The name Nimrod means rebellion and the Hebrew word for Babel is the same for the word Babylon. If we substitute the word "Kingdom" with the word "State"—and I think we can without twisting the meaning of either word—we can see that Babylon is a symbol for the State from Genesis 10 all the way up to Revelation 19—and Babylon is always a symbol of *opposition* against the people of God. The Old Testament record speaks loud and clear that God sees the institution of the State as an act of rebellion!

So why did God create a nation/state under the Old Covenant with the children of Israel? I believe it was so that He could provide humanity with an object lesson to expose the inadequacy of the State as an instrument for achieving moral ends. All earthly kingdoms are built on violence—even God *ordained* earthly kingdoms! God started the theocracy experiment with Moses. Then He played the part of a tribal war god and ordered the slaughtering of the Canaanites to show that if you're going to deal with evil by violent means, then you have to go all the way. Still, power was largely decentralized until we get to 1 Samuel 8 when the Israelites demanded a king. According to the prophet Samuel, God saw the centralization of power as an act of rebellion, but He went along with it anyway—reluctantly. There were a few good kings in the mix like David, Hezekiah, and Josiah, but most of them were despicable tyrants. After the kingdom divided, God sent prophet after prophet to condemn the kings for oppressing their people and—a bit of irony for today's Christian Zionists—trusting in their military might. The Assyrians eventually gobbled up the ten tribes of Israel and shortly afterwards the tribe of Judah was taken captive by Babylon. Finally, He sent His one and only Son to offer the Jewish people a transnational Kingdom based on non-violent redemptive love—and the rest is history.

What happened in 70 A.D. in the destruction of the Jewish temple was the ultimate vindication of Christ and His non-violent new world order. Jesus chose to establish the Kingdom of God through suffering redemptive love and was gloriously resurrected on the third day. The Jews on the other hand clanged to their tradition of violence and nationalism and ended up suffering a crushing defeat by the Romans. If we look at what happened in 70 A.D. and view it through the lens of the Old Testament narrative, then we have to conclude *that even God ordained theocracies* are unable to establish the Kingdom of God on earth. Violence and nationalism can never bring in the Kingdom of God and *that was the point all along!* Just like the Jewish Law was a negative object lesson to demonstrate the impossibility of justification by works, so the

Jewish theocracy of the Old Testament was a negative object lesson to demonstrate that God's kingdom can never be established by violent means!

The Bible when understood in its entirety is an anti-war, anti-nationalist document. In the Old Testament, we see glimpses of a peace-loving God that's in the business of "making wars cease to the ends of the earth" (Ps 46:9), of a God that doesn't want people to delight in war (Psalm 68:30) of a God that refuses to live in temples built by hands that shed blood (I Chronicles 22:8), of a God that sets apart a people for priestly service and forbids them to join the military (Numbers 1), of a God that shows mercy to violent criminals (Genesis 4:15, 2 Chronicles 43:10–17, Jonah 4:1–11), but it's not till we get to Jesus that we see a God that takes on the form of a human being; more specifically, a human being that rejected earthly power structures—and taught His followers to do the same.

When Jesus took a towel and washed His disciples' mud-encrusted feet, He wasn't just *redefining* earthly power; He was *rejecting* earthly power. By taking on the form of a slave, Jesus forever elevated the status of the powerless over the powerful—just like His mother did (Luke 1:51–53). The act of washing His disciples' feet was a prophetic act that symbolized the way *things are supposed to be*—like the way it was in the Garden of Eden when human beings didn't rule over each other, but loved and served each other. Jesus taught His followers that the system of dominion and authority was for Gentiles, not for the newly constituted people of God (Matthew 20:26–27).

The New Testament Church is called to model equality by creating a society of men and women practicing the *one anothers* of Christian brotherhood. In Christ, there is neither Jew nor Gentile, slave nor free, male nor female. All are one. (Galatians 3:28) This doesn't mean that individual Christians can't function in some degree of authority over others outside of their respective callings in the church, but it does mean that Christians are supposed to consider their unique calling to servant-hood when considering earthly occupations.

The Apostle Paul could conceive of a Christian husband serving his wife in loving humility; he could also conceive of a Christian master treating his slave like a brother—much like a good employer could treat an employee in our own time—but the odd thing is it seems that Paul could *not* conceive of a Christian king. John Howard Yoder writes about this curious detail in Paul's Haustafelh—which is a fancy word for household code—in his book *Politics of Jesus*:

"There is one striking difference, however, at this point. After the invitation to wives we saw that the Haustafeln addressed a similar and immensely more novel call to husbands to love their wives; after calling slaves to be subject, the early Christian moralists called upon the masters to be equally respectful; after calling children to remain subordinate to parents, the admonition was turned about and addressed to parents as well. When, however, the call to subordination is addressed to the Christian in his status as a political subject, in these texts the exhortation is not reversed. There is no invitation to the king to conceive of himself as a public servant. Was this only because, as a matter of course, the apostolic preachers and authors recognized that there were no kings in their audiences? Or was it that, in line with the teaching of Christ, which had been preserved in several forms, Jesus had instructed his disciples specifically to reject governmental domination over others as unworthy of the disciple's calling of servant-hood?"

Unlike the first three centuries of church history, most Christians today are uneasy with the idea that following Jesus precludes accepting certain positions of governmental authority over others, but as long as we're in the business of taking Jesus seriously, shouldn't we at least *consider* that Jesus' elevation of the slave over the master, the poor over the rich, the last over the first, and the towel over the sword was a model He intended His followers to imitate? Throughout His earthly ministry, Jesus *consistently* eschewed earthly power as a means of controlling other people's behavior. Jesus *never* displayed an interest in overthrowing existing power institutions—or even acquiring power so that He could reform them.

This doesn't mean that Jesus was apolitical, as if Jesus was only concerned with spiritual matters and not with matters of social concern. Not at all! Jesus was *very* political, but what the vast majority of Christians today fail to realize is Jesus was political in an anarchist sort of way. Jesus never subordinated His conscience to another human being regardless of whatever positions of power they held. When Jesus cleansed the temple, He not only challenged the political, religious, and financial authority of His day; He *deliberately disrupted* their activity. If we put the cleansing of the temple in the context of it's time, the cleansing of the temple was an *extremely* political act aimed at challenging the central axis of unjust power in His day. Jesus was an activist *par excellence* for the interests of the poor and the marginalized.

The reason why both Jesus *and Paul* (Romans 12:14–21, I Thessalonians 5:15) forbade Christians the use of the sword is because when Christians use the sword, we undermine our unique calling to be a prophetic people that embody the reality of the age to come (Hebrews 6:5). In the age to come, "Nation will not lift up sword against nation, and neither will they learn war any more" (Isaiah 2:4, Micah 4:3). In the age to come, the meek are going to inherit the earth (Matthew 5:5). People won't be ruling over each other, but serving each other in self-sacrificial love—like Jesus did. When Jesus preached that the Kingdom of God is at hand, He was calling forth a people from the north, the south, the east, and the west to live in the reality of the age to come in the here and now.

When Martin Luther launched the protestant reformation in 1517, establishing justification by faith apart from works, he was absolutely right to do so—but the reformation didn't go far enough. The real reformers were the Anabaptists that believed in a strict separation between Church and State and renounced all violence as contrary to the Christian call to servant-hood. The tragedy of the 20th century is that a group of people called Pentecostals started out the same way—and paid a dear price for it when some of them were thrown in prison for refusing to fight in World War I—but when the temptation came to embrace the sword over the cross, the Pentecostals and their charismatic godchildren didn't just nibble at the bait. We devoured the bait.

My concern isn't just for society, but for the Body of Christ. At the time of this writing, President George W. Bush has one of the lowest approval ratings in history. Right or wrong, this puts an enormous barrier in the way for people that are thirsty for spiritual truth, but feel that if they join an evangelical church, they're joining a group of people plunging the country in the wrong direction. Rather than pimping Caesar to control other people's behavior for us, I wonder what the Church worldwide would look like if it were universally agreed upon that our *only* moral agenda in this world is to imitate Jesus? What if our *only* moral agenda was to love people, serve people, and meet their needs— no questions asked. What if we followed the example of Jesus and refused to embrace earthly power over others? What if we elevated the towel over the sword like Jesus did? What if we became a people that separated ourselves from worldly power institutions *so that* we can devote ourselves to doing good works to serve our fellow man? (Ephesians 2:10) What if instead of going to seminars and spending millions of dollars every year to make ourselves *relevant*, we devoted the same time and resources to making ourselves *peculiar*? (Titus 2:14, 1 Peter 2:9)

I long for the day when a conversation like this could take place.

"Dad, can I talk to you about something?"

"Yeah, son, what's on your mind?"

"I want to ask you about a group of people that I've always been curious about. They don't serve in the military, but they donate cell phones to help soldiers contact their families. They pay their taxes but they refuse to invest in companies that manufacture weapons. They refuse to defend themselves by carrying a gun but they don't seem to be interested in overturning the second amendment. They refuse to pledge allegiance to the State, but they teach their children to obey the laws of the land. Their leaders say that abortion is a sin, but they're the first ones to offer love and forgiveness to women who've had abortions—and they start homes for unwed mothers. They say that sex is supposed to be reserved for marriage between a man and a woman, but then they hand out water at gay parades and work tirelessly to relieve the suffering of aids victims. A few of them live in communities where they share possessions and have things in common, but all of them strive to live simply so that others can simply live. And Dad, you know the guy that just took over Nike? The one that reformed the sweat shops in Indonesia and donated all but a small percentage of his multi-million dollar salary to help his employees' children go to college? He said that he's been born again and now he's one of them too. Why would somebody do a thing like that?"

"Well, son. I've been meaning to talk to you about that. Those people that you're referring to are called Christians. Lately I've been thinking about joining them. They say they follow a Jewish carpenter that died a couple of thousand years ago on a wooden cross, but was miraculously resurrected on the third day. They say that if you trust in Him, your sins will be forgiven and you'll get to walk beside Him in a new heaven and a new earth one day. They have this initiation ritual where they dunk people in water to symbolize death to the old way of life and resurrection to the new. I've been thinking about taking the plunge, but I don't want to do it alone. What do you say we take the plunge together?"

"Dad. I couldn't think of anything that would make me happier. With all that's gone wrong in the world, I'd like to be a part of the answer, not a part of the problem."

After the second day of my debate with Khalid, I took a train back to the house of an old friend from Bible School that was kind enough to host me for the week. As I stared into the cold damp night, passing from station to station, it felt like the weight of the world was pressing on my shoulders. I knew that if there was to be any victory like the one prophesied by the man that walked up to me at a Pentecostal church in Brazil, then I'd have to keep digging until I found a response to Khalid's primary moral objection to Christianity. Why *didn't* Jesus leave us with a socio-political system to govern society as Muhammad attempted to do? Why didn't Jesus teach His followers to seize the reigns of political institutions so they could make God's law the law of the land—as Moses before Him had done? In an age of nuclear proliferation, environmental degradation, and devastating inequality between the global north and the global south, wouldn't it be nice if humanity could have a step by step instruction book for how to implement global utopia—like the Muslims claim that they have?

It's been well over a year now since my debate with Khalid and I've finally reached the conclusion of the matter. No Jesus didn't leave the world with a socio-political system to solve its problems. What He gave us instead was the cross. At the cross, Jesus taught humanity that it's better to suffer injustice than to be the cause of it, it's better to relinquish power than to pursue power, and, perhaps most importantly, it's better to die than to kill. By rejecting earthly power, Jesus introduced to the world a model for a new kind of human being—the model of a powerless prophet.

Moses dreamed of a day when all God's people would prophesy, and that's precisely what happened on the day of Pentecost. God created a company of prophets to serve as a witness to the world of the reality of the age to come. Like the Hebrew prophets of old, the Church is called to be a company of prophets that embrace powerlessness so that they can confront the powerful. James the brother of the Lord Jesus never wielded the power of the sword through political office, but in an age when C.E.O.s make four hundred times the salary an average worker makes in a day, the words of this powerless prophet speak with crushing clarity:

"Come now, you rich, weep and howl for your miseries that are coming upon you! Your riches are corrupted, and your garments are moth-eaten. Your gold and silver are corroded, and their corrosion will be a witness against you and will eat your flesh like fire. You have heaped up treasure in the last days. Indeed the wages of the laborers who mowed your fields, which you kept back by fraud, cry out; and the cries of the reapers have reached the ears of the Lord of Sabaoth. You have lived on the earth in pleasure and luxury, you have fattened your hearts as in a day of slaughter. You have condemned, you have murdered the just; he does not resist you" (James 5:1–6).

No matter how many times the leaders of worldly kingdoms claim that their wars are fought for righteous purposes, Kingdom of God citizens know better. The real source of war is covetousness (James 4:1–2). Never was this made clearer to me than the day after my debate with Khalid when I visited the British Museum and saw a display that lodged itself into the deep recesses of my heart and refuses to let me go. For decades, America and the Soviet Union had been pouring weapons into the country of Mozambique, fueling the senseless slaughter of Africans as part of their cold war chess match. Though it seemed that the killing had no end in sight, one day a Christian group from Italy called the San Egidio community showed up and patiently worked with both sides until they agreed to stop killing each other. The display was of a tree made not of wood, but of guns that had been exchanged for agricultural tools. As I saw how instruments of death could be transformed into such a beautiful work of art, I stood and wept—and then dedicated myself to the art of peace-making.

There's coming a day when every man, woman, and child will beat their swords into plowshares and their spears into pruning hooks. But why wait till the age to come? The world is crying out for peace today. Let there be peace on earth—and for the love of God—let it begin with the Church!

Brief answers to tough questions

I t's been almost two years since my time with Khalid in an old abandoned warehouse. Stephen Marshall, the director of Holy Wars is working around the clock to get the film ready to submit to the Sundance Film Festival. It's hard to believe that it's been two and half years since I first answered that e-mail looking for a young missionary that travels the world to partici-pate in a feature length documentary. I started out with the hope that perhaps in some way I could undo some of the negative stereotypes in the media that have plagued the evangelical world over the past few decades. The last thing I expected was that I'd end up dramatically changed in the process. I have no idea if this film will ever get off the ground. Maybe it will. Maybe it won't. The funny thing is now that I've learned what I needed to learn, it doesn't seem to matter to me as much as it did in the beginning. I figure that if God can knock a self-righteous Pharisee like Saul off a horse to get his attention, then certainly He can arrange a meeting in an old abandoned warehouse between a radical jihadist and a Christian missionary to force the missionary to consider the implications of the gospel he's been preaching for half his life.

I started writing this book 16 months ago—about four months after my encounter with Khalid. When I originally started writing I had no idea where my thought process would take me. It all started with the simple idea that Jesus never left a system of government in place, therefore any attempt to equate an earthly system—be it democracy, capitalism, socialism, or any other "ism" out there— with the kingdom of God is misguided. It was this idea that caused me to question the wisdom of Christians rallying behind an agenda to export an "ism" to the world at the barrel of a gun—even if it's an American "ism."

Before I knew it I began to think about the role that religion often plays in rallying peoples and nations to war. A book I read early on was Samuel Huntington's *The Clash of Civilizations and the Remaking of World Order*. Though the book was written in 1996, Huntington predicted that unlike the cold war era where the bulk of wars were fought over political and economic philosophies, the post cold-war era would be marked by religious wars. Huntington's thesis was—and still is—very controversial in foreign policy circles, but the underlying dangers of fusing religion with national identity remain the same.

As much as I'd like to think that it's possible to answer every possible objection to the pacifist position that I'm advocating in this book (also known as Christian anarchist and/or Biblical non-resistance), I know that it took me a very long time to arrive at this conclusion. I think it's safe to say that I entered the pacifist world kicking and screaming, so I know how very hard it is to undo an entire lifetime of cultural conditioning. That being said, I'm not the type of person that likes to leave stones unturned, so I've provided brief answers to some of the most emotionally and intellectually challenging objections to Biblical pacifism.

1. You argue for absolute non-violence on the part of a Christian, but you live in a country that gives you the freedom to obey your conscience, and that freedom was bought and paid for by the sacrifice of others who gave their lives to fight for that freedom. How do you justify living off the sacrifice of others?

This is by *far* the most emotionally charged objection to Biblical pacifism. The argument seems to suggest that pacifists are little more than parasites living off the sacrifices of the rest of society. What disturbs me the most about this objection is how often it's raised by *Christians* that seem to think this is the argument that ends the discussion regardless of what the Bible has to say about the subject. Need I say the obvious? If the Bible teaches that followers of Jesus are never supposed to support, advocate, or execute the killing of another human being, then the only thing that matters is what God says about the issue, not what man says. Having said that, I realize that every doctrine must pass the moral test, so I offer a few insights here.

First of all, the argument suggests that had the various wars fought by the U.S. military never taken place, then America wouldn't be a free nation today. Americans wouldn't have the right to vote and neither would we have the right to worship freely. Ask any American from the age of 5 to 99 why soldiers in America fight and the answer you'll almost always hear is Americans fight for freedom. The idea that we owe our freedom to our military might is so ingrained in American thinking that *very* few dare to question it. But question it we must. As healthy as a patriotic spirit can be, patriotism can easily be exploited by politicians eager to pursue an imperial agenda.

Is it really true that had the U.S. never invaded Vietnam, then none of us would have the right to vote or worship freely? How about the invasion of the Philippines? Gulf One? The Mexican War? What if the U.S. had remained neutral in World War One? Would there have been a World War II? Is it true that we wouldn't be a free nation if colonists had never rebelled against Great Britain? As I argued in chapter 5, Australia and Canada are free nations today and they never engaged in violent revolution. Great Britain transitioned from a monarchy to a democracy without a single drop of blood. Violence isn't the only way to achieve political freedom.

Secondly—and I find this inexcusable—the argument overlooks entirely the contribution that pacifist Christians have made throughout the centuries toward the cause of human freedom. As long as we're talking about freedom, let's talk about religious free-dom. Religious freedom is the foundation upon which every other freedom lays. Do the roots of religious freedom lie at the barrel of a gun? Hardly. The roots of religious freedom lie with the Anabaptists of the 16th century.

The Anabaptists believed that all warfare and killing is wrong and because of this position they refused to bear arms, fight in wars, or participate in wielding the power of the sword in any way, shape, or form. It's precisely the Anabaptist vision of a separation of Church and State that became the foundation of Western democracy. Many of the early Anabaptists were put to death for their faith—often by the hands of their protestant brothers that took their cues less from Jesus and more from Augustine. The truth of the matter is this. Much of the freedom that we now enjoy is due to the blood of the Anabaptist martyrs of the 16th century. How sad that these precious martyrs' contribution to freedom is so often despised!

Thirdly, there are many other ways to contribute to the health of a society without participating in institutions that take human life. I'm not advocating that Christians withdraw from sword-wielding institutions just for the sake of withdrawal. I'm advocating that we withdraw from these institutions *so that* we can spend our creative energy on preaching the gospel and serving our fellow man through good works. By exchanging the sword for the towel, followers of Jesus model to the world what life will look like in the age to come. If we ask the question of what the world would look like if *everyone* renounced violence and lived by an ethic of suffering redemptive love, then the pacifist position passes the moral test with flying colors. Though we recognize the sword wielding power of the State as a legitimate function in a fallen human race, the role of the Church is to witness to a higher reality that will be fully manifest in the age to come.

2. You say that violence is wrong for a Christian, and yet you recognize that judges, legislators, the police, and sometimes the military serve a useful function for society. Are you saying that God has one standard for Christians and another for non-Christians?

As I wrote in chapter 7, the question of whether a Christian should serve as a judge, a legislator, on the police force, or in certain non-combatant roles in military service is an open one. Among the historic peace churches, there's a considerable amount of variation in terms of what's allowable as a legitimate occupation for a Christian. For example, among the Mennonites (the modern descendants of the Anabaptists) it's rare to see a Mennonite serve in an official government capacity that requires the use of force (like a police officer or a legislator), even though the Mennonite denomination leaves a considerable degree up to the individual conscience to decide. Although you may find an occasional Mennonite police officer or mayor, it's universally agreed in the Mennonite denomination that a Christian can never participate in the death penalty nor serve in military combat.

As to the charge that I'm saying that God has one standard for some and a different standard for others, my answer is: Well, what if I am? Biblically speaking, it's not unheard of to say that God holds some people to a higher standard than others (Luke 12:48, James 3:1). That being said, it doesn't necessarily follow that

God's revelation in Jesus is any different from the moral law as revealed in the 10 commandments which applies to all people at all times. One of the 10 commandments is "Thou shalt not kill." Jesus expounded on this idea in the Sermon on the Mount when He said, "You have heard that it was said, 'an eye for an eye and a tooth for a tooth, but I tell you not to resist an evil person" (Matthew 5:38–39). Here Jesus rejects the tit for tat ways of the world and upholds the intent of the moral law as revealed in the 10 commandments that doesn't allow for the killing of another human being *even as retribution.* Also consider that the one and only time Jesus was questioned about the death penalty, He said, "He who is without sin among you, let him cast the first stone" (John 8:7).

Why does God seem to contradict Himself by prescribing the death penalty in the Old Testament? Very simple. The death penalty was a part of the *civil* law that, according to Jesus, some aspects of the civil law were given as an accommodation to human sinfulness (Matthew 19:8, Mark 10:5). While I think it's safe to say that God judges people based on the light that they have (Luke 12:48), that doesn't change the fact that the moral life of Christ is the ultimate standard by which everyone will be judged. Once we understand that the life of Christ is the moral standard by which everyone is judged, then we can safely conclude that the power of the sword may be a necessary evil, but it's still an evil nonetheless—even if it's a lesser evil than those who kill for less noble purposes.

3. In Matthew 5:38–39, 43–48 Jesus is teaching against taking personal vengeance against those who have wronged you. He's not talking about legal vengeance. All Jesus is saying is not to have hatred in your heart for other people.

Wrong. Christ's reference to "An eye for an eye and a tooth for a tooth" is clearly a reference to the *legal* method of avenging an offense under the civil law of Moses. Even in the Law of Moses, personal vengeance was forbidden. A person had to take the offender to a civil magistrate to administer the legal retribution (which was always in exact proportion to the crime) and *even then* there had to be two to three witnesses before the punishment could be administered (Deuteronomy 17:6). What Jesus is saying here is that a Christian must not appeal to the state for revenge against offenders? [41] There's simply no way of getting around the plain teachings of Jesus on this matter.

As to the charge that Jesus is merely talking about removing hatred from human hearts and isn't prescribing anything in terms of an actual change in behavior, does it really make a difference to an innocent civilian that's been killed in a bombing raid if the one dropping the bomb held malice in his or her heart? Is the person any less dead? At least hatred is directed towards *persons*. A person who can kill without feeling *anything* may be in a worse spiritual condition than the person that at least feels something. That's essentially the moral problem that makes war intrinsically evil. War depersonalizes human beings by turning them into dispensable commodities. The ends don't justify the means.

---

41 *War, Peace, and Non-Resistance* (Herald Press 1944,1953,1969), 51

4. What would you do if you saw someone attacking a member of your family or an innocent child? Certainly you'd be justified to respond with lethal violence in an instance like that wouldn't you?

No. Jesus never once qualified His statements about not resisting evil with violence. Having said that, I'm not sure exactly how I would respond if faced with a threatening situation to my family. My flesh may lash out at someone, but I am hopeful my convictions would temper my fleshly response. Jesus rebuked Peter for using the sword even though Peter's intentions were to protect the innocent. When Jesus was faced with a violent mob that was about to thrust Him—and perhaps His disciples—off a cliff, His very presence awed the crowd to the point that He was able to pass through the midst of them unharmed (Luke 4:29–30). Just because I can't imagine *Jesus* responding to extreme situations with violence doesn't mean I know that's what I would do in a situation like that. I'd love to be able to pull off a passing through the crowd stunt, but I know that it takes a considerable degree of cultivating a Christ-like spirit to diffuse a situation the way Jesus would. Nevertheless, I do believe this degree of Christ-likeness is attainable, though I would never condemn myself or others who fail to meet this standard. If I know anything about the Father heart of God, I'm reasonably certain that God would understand too (Psalms 103:14).

Having said that, non-violence certainly doesn't mean do nothing. Too often the word pacifism has been taken to mean *passivity*, but nothing can be further from the truth. As Christians, we've been given the twin weapons of the Word of God and prayer. We have authority in the name of Jesus to speak to difficult situations and command them to change, especially if demonic spirits are involved (calling all Pentecostals!) Of course, there are also practical ways of diffusing violent situations and many times, doing the unexpected is exactly what it takes to change the dynamics of a violent situation. I like Shane Claibourne's idea of clucking like a chicken, but if that doesn't work, there's a myriad of ways in which the Holy Spirit could direct a Christian to behave in extreme situations. That's why Christians need to cultivate a Christ-like spirit on a daily basis.

Perhaps the worst assumption of this question is that the *only* possible outcome of a violent intervention is the rescue of the innocent. The assumption is either you respond violently or the innocent victim dies. The problem with this view is reality is often more complicated than hypothetical formulas. Sometimes reacting violently to an extreme situation can actually *worsen* the situation, but this is never taken into account when this question is asked. What if the moment you pull out the gun or strike a punch the attacker decides to intensify or hasten what they're doing and kills you *and the innocent victim* in the process? As long as we're dealing with hypothetical situations, there's nothing sacred about a violent response to an extreme situation that guarantees a positive outcome any more than a non-violent response, so why not aim for a non-violent response?

Lastly, regardless of the stand an individual takes on the question of what to do in extreme situations like warding off an individual attacker, it should be noted that this question has no bearing at all on whether a Christian should participate in war. If a violent attacker attacks my family or me, nobody in his or her right mind would say that I have a moral right to kill the attacker's mother or family in retaliation. Neither would anybody say that I have a right to enter the attacker's neighborhood and take over people's homes, killing whoever I please—as long as it's not intentional—to defend my wife and children. And yet this is *exactly* what happens in war. Collateral damage isn't *accidental*. In modern warfare, it's *inevitable*. And the deaths are almost always in the thousands. Why do we call an action criminal when perpetrated by an individual but courageous when perpetrated by a group?

5. What about situations like Darfur where innocent people are being slaughtered by government sponsored militias or situations like Myanmar where tyrannical governments actively target minority groups for ethnic cleansing? Shouldn't Christians use the sword to defend the innocent in cases like these?

I dealt with this briefly in chapter seven, so I won't rehash the same arguments I made in that chapter here, though I would like to add a few extra points of clarification. First of all, a commitment to non-violence does *not* mean that a Christian has to take the position that every act of killing is morally equivalent—as if Rambo were morally equivalent to Jack the Ripper. The position that I'm advocating is that God has a unique role for the Church in the world and it's because of the uniqueness of this calling that a Christian is forbidden to take up arms or wield the power of the sword. But this doesn't mean do *nothing!* Extreme situations demand a moral response, so the question becomes what is the appropriate moral response for a Christian to extreme questions like terrorism or ethnic cleansing?

The first line of response for a Christian should *always* be to trust in the resources of the twin weapons of the Word of God and prayer. God has entrusted us with the gospel of reconciliation, and it's precisely the gospel of reconciliation that is so desperately needed in extreme situations where people are suffering. The gospel of Jesus Christ is the only power in this world that has the power to bring healing to the sufferer *and* repentance to the oppressor. I've read some exciting testimonies from missionary groups that are in Sudan right now sharing the love of Jesus on both sides of the conflict. So the question I'd like to ask in return is since when is preaching the gospel doing nothing?

Secondly, Christians can certainly reach out to those suffering in war torn countries in humanitarian ways and in no way should we underestimate the powerful effect this can have. Often just the very presence of missionaries and/or humanitarian workers in war torn countries can go a long way in drawing the world's attention to the plight of those suffering in extreme situations. On a similar note, it's important to understand that there's nothing in the Biblical pacifist position that forbids a Christian from speaking truth to power about injustices around the world. As a matter of fact, we're *called* to this! One of the New Testament mandates for a Christian is to expose the works of darkness (Ephesians 5:11). By drawing attention to extreme situations through united prayer efforts, sending missionaries, relieving the suffering through humanitarian efforts, speaking to the media, conducting corporate responsibility campaigns, and speaking to government officials when appropriate, Christians can go a long way in exposing the works of darkness. Once we do our part by focusing on the ends, we can leave it up to responsible government officials to determine the means by which to handle the situation.

Thirdly, although I feel it's best for Christians to draw attention to the world's suffering by focusing more on ends and less on means, that doesn't mean that a few politically savvy Christians can't make sound policy recommendations to the proper government officials. Of course, a Christian would want to recommend a wide variety of diplomatic solutions to pressure oppressive regimes to lay down their arms. Sometimes this could include carefully targeted sanctions, setting up governments in exile, divestment campaigns from corporations that profit from tyrannical governments, turning over government leaders guilty of war crimes to the International Criminal Court, and a host of other options.

Finally, I think there's merit to the argument that pacifists that oppose war should propose alternatives, so if after all diplomatic options are exhausted and a Christian absolutely *has* to propose the use of force; the proposal should always be a *limited* use of force that's clearly defined by legal boundaries. One such alternative is that of an international police force proposed by Jim Wallis of Sojourners. Under the guidance of an internationally recognized body like the U.N., a global police force would be a legitimate authority capable of arresting terrorists and war criminals and bringing them to justice under international law. Former Secretary of State Madeline Albright in her book *The Mighty and the Almighty* also recommends an international police force—as opposed to a standing army—as an effective means of dealing with terrorism and war crimes.

Interestingly, a recent study by the Rand Corporation, a highly influential non-partisan think tank, suggests that the war on terror is better waged by law enforcement than by armies. [42] Such an approach would be far more cost effective than the 400 billion dollars a year our nation's congress spends on an over-bloated military budget. Just *a fraction* of the savings alone could repair our nations' crumbling roads and bridges, fund desperately needed reform to America's education and health care system, eliminate our need for middle east oil, and feed the world's 6 million starving children. [43]

6. Jesus said, "Render unto Caesar the things that belong to Caesar." Part of rendering unto Caesar the things that belong to Caesar is military service to defend one's country.

The problem with this argument is it takes Jesus' words completely out of context. The Pharisees that questioned Jesus on this matter

---

42 http://www.washingtonpost.com/wp-dyn/content/article
/2008/07/29/AR2008072902041.html
Accessed August 5th, 2008

43 Ben Cohen, the founder of Ben and Jerry's ice cream has a funny cartoon on the internet that illustrates this point.
You can watch it at http://www.truemajority.com/oreos/

were certainly not interested in serving in the Roman army. If anything, they would have been interested in overthrowing the Roman government. By telling His questioners to pay their taxes to Caesar, His point was that they shouldn't rebel against the Romans. Jesus is actually teaching non-resistance in this passage, not the opposite. Also notice the ambiguity of the answer. The answer begs the question, "What belongs to Caesar?" By adding the phrase, "But to God the things that are God's," Jesus anticipated that sometimes the demands of Caesar would be contradictory to the demands of God. Since the New Testament clearly teaches that followers of Jesus are to resist not evil, turn the other cheek, and never execute vengeance, when it comes to matters of sword-wielding power, Christians are to obey God, not Caesar.

7. Jesus said, "Do not think that I came to bring peace on earth. I did not come to bring peace but a sword." (Matthew 10:34) Jesus did in fact advocate the use of the sword for Christians.

Jesus is not advocating violence in this passage. If we look at the verse that follows, we can see that Jesus is predicting that His followers would suffer trials as a result of their faith. Jesus predicted that His message would divide families, setting sons against fathers, daughters against mothers, and daughter in laws against mother in laws (Vs 35). Everywhere the gospel is preached, it brings division. The sword that Jesus is talking about in this passage is the sword of tribulation experienced by Christians throughout the centuries that have suffered for their faith.

8. Jesus told the disciples to purchase a sword, and when the disciples showed Him two swords, He said, "It is enough." (Luke 22:36–38) Wasn't Jesus telling His disciples that they would need swords to defend themselves?

No. We know this because when Peter actually tried to use the sword, Jesus told Him to put his sword back in his place and further rebuked him with the words, "All that take the sword will perish by the sword." While this verse is admittedly difficult, it should not undermine the overwhelming testimony that Jesus taught non-resistance in the face of evil. Also consider that two swords would not have been enough for the disciples to defend Him against an entire mob that came to arrest Him. As far as what Jesus meant by the words "It is enough," I find Jack Hayford's commentary footnote in the Spirit Filled Life Bible satisfactory:

"The words 'it is enough' do not mean, "They are sufficient." They are a curt dismissal of the subject, in the sense of "Enough of that!"

Another interpretation of this passage is that Jesus use of the two swords was meant to be a symbolic enactment of Isaiah's prophecy that said Jesus would be numbered with the transgressors. Jesus refers to this passage directly before the disciples went to look for the swords (Vs 37).

Whatever this passage means, it has to be examined within the context of Jesus' entire life and ministry. Jesus refused violence at every opportunity, and taught His followers to do the same.

9. Didn't Jesus use a scourge of whips to drive the money-changers out of the temple? (John 2:15)

Yes, Jesus made a scourge of whips, but notice that the verse doesn't say that Jesus actually *used* the scourge of whips. Even if we grant that Jesus actually used the scourge of whips, verse 14 makes it clear that He used it not on the men, but on the sheep and the oxen. Had Jesus actually used physical violence on the men, then certainly the act would have provoked a violent reaction, something we don't see in this passage.

10. What about the military illustrations in Jesus' parables? Doesn't that mean that Jesus condoned warfare?

The parables in question are found in Matthew 22:7, Luke 11:21, and Luke 14:31. In the parable of the wedding feast, after the invitees kill the kings' servants, the king sends an army to destroy the murderers and burn down their city. This is an obvious reference to the destruction of Jerusalem that took place in 70 A.D. Far from advocating violence in this passage; Jesus is warning His listeners of the disastrous consequences the Jewish nation would face for rejecting His message. As to Luke 11:21, this parable is hardly an endorsement of violence since the strong man that guards his palace is a reference to *Satan*—and the point of the passage is that Jesus is stronger.

As to the example of Luke 14:31 where Jesus describes a king evaluating whether or not he has the sufficient number of troops to make war against another king, the point of the passage is that people need to count the cost before deciding to follow Jesus.

The military imagery is simply for the purpose of illustration and is not an endorsement for war. In the parables of Jesus, the details of the illustrations are always incidental to the main point. In this case, the main point of the passage is hardly an endorsement of violence. In fact, the opposite is true. The point of the parable is found in verse 33 where Jesus says, "So likewise, whoever of you does not forsake all that he has cannot be My disciple." Jesus is saying that His followers should be willing to sacrifice their lives for the cause of the gospel, even if that means forsaking possessions and enduring martyrdom. Laying down one's life for the cause of the gospel is a far cry from taking another life in an act of war.

11. Revelation 19:15 portrays Jesus as a conquering warrior. This shows that Jesus approves of war. Christians that take the sword are merely following the example of their Lord.

First of all, I should mention that there are a wide variety of interpretations of this passage. Some say that this is a reference to the wrath of God poured out on the unrighteous at the end of the age. Others say it's a reference to the fall of Jerusalem in 70 A.D. Regardless of which interpretation is correct, there's no contradiction between the doctrine of Biblical pacifism and the idea that God will one day judge the sin of the world. The New Testament makes it crystal clear that vengeance is *God's* prerogative, not man's prerogative. That Jesus will judge the world at the end of the age in no way negates the fact that Christians are never supposed to participate in acts of vengeance against evil-doers. As the Apostle Paul writes in Romans 12:19, "Beloved, do not avenge yourselves, but rather give place to wrath; for it is written, 'Vengeance is Mine, I will repay,' says the Lord."

12. Jesus said, "Greater love have no man than this that one lay down his life for his friends." Soldiers who give their lives in war manifest the greatest possible love for mankind.

This verse is a favorite for army chaplains. Some even go as far as to compare the sacrifice of a soldier that gives his life in war with the sacrifice that Jesus made on the cross. This is blasphemy! While it's true that followers of Jesus should be willing to sacrifice their lives for the sake of others, there's nothing in this passage that approves of killing other human beings in the process. A soldier's first objective is to kill his enemies, not to lay down his life. The objective of soldiers is to make it so that the guys on the other side sacrifice *their* lives. Followers of Jesus, on the other hand, are called to imitate the cross—where Jesus died for His friends *and* for His enemies.

13. The Hall of Faith passage in Hebrews 11:30–40 honors Old Testament warriors who were valiant in battle. Christians should follow their example.

The point of this passage is that followers of Jesus should honor the *faith* of Old Testament characters. It doesn't mean that we should necessarily imitate their actions. Old Testament heroes like Gideon, Barak, Samson, Jepthah, David, Samuel, and the prophets were faithful to the will of God *as it was revealed to them in their time*. Now that Jesus has come, Christians are to imitate and follow *His* example and teachings. It's helpful to understand that those living in Old Testament times didn't have access to the spiritual resources that are available to Christians under the New Covenant. Under the New Covenant, believers have access to the authority invested in the name of Jesus to deal with the spiritual roots behind wickedness on the earth—something that the Old Testament warriors did not have.

While we're on the subject of Old Testament heroes, why not discuss the example of Elisha? One of the greatest examples of showing kindness and compassion to one's enemies is a story found in 2 Kings 6:18–23. When a band of Syrians came to capture Elisha, rather than calling fire down from heaven as Elijah had done in the past, Elisha struck the men with blindness, led them to Samaria, and then prepared a feast for them! Elisha's act of kindness had a demonstrable effect. Verse 23 makes the point that after Elisha sent the men back to their master; the band of raiders no more came into the land of Israel. Even in Old Testament times the principle of repaying good for evil melted the hearts of violent criminals!

14. I respect your position on non-violence, but I think it's a non-essential. Christians can disagree on this and still be brothers and sisters in Christ.

Oh how I wish I could conclude that the relationship between a Christian and warfare and killing is a nonessential issue! How much easier that would make my life! It's not that I don't appreciate those who love God, go to church, and tolerate my pacifist views with gentleness and grace. I realize that my position though at one time was the majority position in the early church, is now a minority position in the larger evangelical world. But as long as I'm being honest, I'm just not convinced that we're dealing with a non-essential issue here. To be a Christian is to confess that Jesus Christ is *Lord* (Romans 10:9) and Jesus said, "Why do you call Me Lord, Lord, and not do the things which I say?" (Luke 6:46) Ultimately, the question comes down to obedience. Either we obey the teachings of Jesus or we don't. As much as I wish He did, Jesus didn't leave any wiggle room on the question of whether a Christian can participate in violence. Jesus says no to killing. Period! The bottom line is do we obey the teachings of Jesus or do we follow the traditions of men? I realize that I'm in no place to judge another man's servant. All I can say is "As for me and my house, we will serve the Lord!"

About the Author

Aaron D. Taylor is the founder of Great Commission Society, an organization dedicated to sharing the love of Christ and serving the persecuted Church. Aaron and his wife Rhiannon graduated from Christ for the Nations School of Missions in May 2001 and together they've traveled the world many times over for the cause of Christ. Aaron and his wife are known for their willingness to take risks and go to places few are willing to go. In November of 2006, Aaron experienced a dramatic encounter with a radical jihadist from London that changed his life forever. Aaron's life story is partially told in the film Holy Wars, a feature length documentary that examines the role of religion in the current clash between the West and Islam.

Index

Also Available
From Foghorn Publishers

GOING INTO THE HOUSE
BY RODNEY A. WINTERS

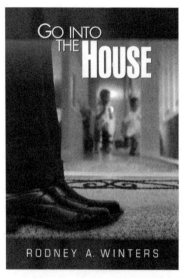

"Not just another book on marriage"

If you wanted to find out how to get rich you probably wouldn't go to a pauper who has never experienced wealth for advice. On the other hand, a person who was born into a wealthy family may not understand the nuts-and-bolts side of building wealth one business at a time.

The best choice for counsel is the person who, through trial and error, has not only gained a sufficient amount of wealth, but has lost it all, and then gained it back again. Such a person will be able to show you how to navigate through your financial journey, avoiding the awful pitfalls along the way. Why is it, when it comes to marriage, that most advice typically comes from people who appear to have never had a down day in their marriage?

Unfortunately, marriages and families are under attack. And they will remain embattled until real solutions come from real people who have gone through fiery tests, yet lived to tell their story. Divorce has long been viewed as an awful difficulty, particularly in the church. The raw truth is that some marriages fail. What happens when your marriage has failed or is close to reaching that point?

Listen to a man who has survived a failed marriage, the scrutiny of the church, and emerged with an honest heartfelt story that will cause you to never see marriage like you did before. Rodney A. Winters isn't sharing a story about love, marriage and divorce that he has heard from someone else. He's lived it. Go into the House, hear what happened, and find out how to prevent the same thing from happening to you.

Whether it's a failed marriage or some other difficulty, we all face some tough decisions at some point after life's disappointments. We must choose to either Go into the House and enjoy the benefits inside, or stay outside and wallow in self-pity. Won't you go inside!

ISBN 10: 1-934466-15-8
ISBN 13: 978-1-934466-15-5

Also Available
From Foghorn Publishers

RELEASING YOUR INNER TREASURE
8 KINGDOM KEYS TO UNLOCKING THE WEALTH WITHIN YOU

BY DR. TECOY PORTER

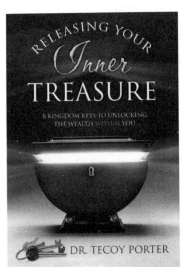

DON'T MISS OUT ON LIFE! Imagine coming to the end of your life and then discovering that you totally missed out on all of the wonderful things that you could have enjoyed. Family vacations, time spent with loved ones, developing your inner self, and even living out your life's purpose all require wealth to some degree. Most people want more of those things in life but settle for life's scraps, believing that a life free of financial worries is only reserved for the uppity ups of society. That is just not true.

The life that you've always dreamed of living, the places that you've always wanted to go, the things that you have wanted to own, and the people that you always wanted to give to are all locked up inside of YOU. That's right your greatest treasure lies deep within you. Dr. Tecoy Porter in Releasing Your Inner Treasure: 8 Kingdom Keys To Unlocking The Wealth Within You will show you how to tap into that sleeping giant, the treasure that lies within you. In this book you will learn:

- How To Condition Your Mind For Millions
- The Power and Purpose of Your Mind and How It Affects Everything In Your Life
- Why You Are The Most Valuable Asset On Earth
- How To Plan Your Way To Riches
- Why Givers Always Get
- The Secret Weapon of Intentional Prayer
- The True Purpose For Money
- How To Get Your Treasure Working For You Instead of Your Treasure Working For The Boss

No more settling for second best! God designed you to live life to the fullest. Everything that pertains to life is already inside of you. Look no further, your greatest gift is not on the way to you, it has already arrived!

ISBN 10: 1-934466-01-8
ISBN 13: 978-1-934466-01-8

The Obama Principle

Creating a Life of Reward through the Power of Perseverance

By Aaron D. Lewis, Ph.D

When you hear comments such as, "He's an overnight success" or "She just rose to stardom from out of nowhere" it makes you really ponder whether statements like those really have any value or if they are true. Do people suddenly appear out of thin air as overnight wonders? Or perhaps is it possible that while no one was watching, certain people were being tested, made, and crafted through though times and the bitter cup of rejection. The truth is; no one just makes it overnight. Whether you realized it or not, the great success stories of life all received their training on the "back side of the dessert" in the so called, "heat of the day."

Using the principle that President Barak Obama has reintroduced to the universe, you too can tackle the most unbelievable accomplishment and win at anything. In The Obama Principle, Aaron D. Lewis will show you how to conquer any dream, through understanding five simple supporting principles. Whether you are a business owner, educator, spiritual leader, politician, stay at home mother, peacemaker, humanitarian, or someone wanting more out of life, these time tested principles will ensure you guaranteed success. Use this winning formula, and embrace the reality that anything is possible.

ISBN 13: 978-1-934466-16-2
ISBN 10: 1-934466-16-6